RELEASE PAIN
From Bondage to Freedom

K. Lee

RELEASE PAIN

Published by Krystal Lee Enterprises (KLE Publishing)
Copyright © 2025 by K. Lee. All rights reserved.
Please send comments and questions:
Krystal Lee Enterprises
770-240-0089 Ext. 1
sales@KLEPub.com
To Reach the Author:
Email: me@drkrystallee.com me@authorklee.com
Web: AuthorKLee.com
Social Media All Channels: @AuthorKLee

The Holy Bible, English Standard Version. ESV® Text Edition: 2016. Copyright © 2001 by Crossway Bibles, a publishing ministry of Good News Publishers. Accessed on Biblegateway.com

Printed in the United States of America.
All rights reserved. No part of this book may be reproduced or transmitted in any form or by any means, electronic or mechanical, including photocopying, recording, or any information storage and retrieval system without written permission of the publisher except for brief quotations used in reviews, written specifically for inclusion in a newspaper, blog, magazine, or academic paper.

ISBN: 978-1-945066-72-6

DEDICATION

     To the lovely people healed by this book and its contents, thank you for allowing me to touch your lives with this powerful message of love and transformation. Special thanks to Kenitra, Yulanda, Paula, TC, Melvina, Kayda, and many more, who encouraged me and allowed me to witness and pray over their lives. Of course, to my Lord and Savior, thank you for giving me a gift to share with the world. I am forever grateful.

Author K Lee

RELEASE PAIN

Contents

Introduction	*5*
Robbery	*10*
Injustice	*38*
Unfaithful	*68*
Betrayal	*100*
Jealousy	*132*
Anger	*162*
Love - Release Pain	*198*
About Author	*212*

INTRODUCTION

If you have been single for a long time, always the bride's maid, not the bride. If you have been overlooked and underestimated. If people have sought ways to use you for your beauty, time, effort, or personality traits like being faithful, honest, and truthful. You've been on single retreats, praying, hoping things will change, and they have not.

If you were standing on the right side of justice, doing what was right and treating others fairly, and they lied on you. If you were the one giving from your heart and sharing your wealth, and now people who you've helped won't give you a thing. Those who should be given to you are still taken and finding ways to guilt-trip you or manipulate you into giving them something else.

If those who were around you were supposed to protect you, but they were the reason you lost your virtue. If you have been drugged, raped, molested, or harmed by people who violated your voice and boundaries. If you have felt empty, dirty, alone, and unloved, take courage, my sister. It can get better.

You are not alone, and the rejection, abuse, and mistreatment of others can lead to problems in your life. This book will uncover the six areas in our lives that can hold a stockpile of trauma-pain. And I want to help you Release Pain.

If you know there are people who have done you wrong. The people who have claimed to love you have turned their backs on you. Sold your heart, stumped on your dreams, and cursed your future; keep turning the pages.

I know it is not easy to forgive people who should have loved you but who didn't. People who should have protected you but instead exposed you. To the many who have had people in their lives find new ways to hurt them, I am here, and I want to take this journey of healing with you.

There are traumatic events that can happen in our lives that leave us believing but feeling defeated. That can give us the will to live but not the faith to believe. If you are stuck in life in a place you know is not where you should be, I want you to know that what you believed for in your past is not too late to believe for again.

I know some of us picked relationships that drug us through the mud, racking our emotions over the coals and singeing our hearts for wanting to love again. We have been hurt by those we loved who stole from us, stealing money, our value, hope, happiness, or the ability to forgive. We need to release this pain.

If you have ever said, "I can never"-forgive, hope, dream, marry again, date, or let people into my inner circle." You need to release pain. Pain will hold your future in limbo for as long as you allow it to trip you up. I would even say demons and evil spirits have many of us bound, and we don't know where to point the finger. Unresolved pain will open six pathways that will have you entangle yourself with doctrines of demons and evil spirits.

INTRODUCTION

If you are not sure how you started to limit your life, what went wrong might not be something you have done but could be something you now believe. I want to help you take this journey, where you can take each step with empowering verses to reform your thoughts, hearts, and patterns and improve your life. You don't have to live your life in pain.

It is possible to endure, but when you are enduring pain with no clear reason for why or how you can limit its influence, it can lead to anger. Anger, unfiltered, is dangerous for anybody. This emotion can have us go on a hellbent path to seek our own vindication, which only leads to more pain. To those who have inflicted pain on others, the weight of guilt and remorse can be mortifying.

A common saying is "Hurt people hurt people," but when we are well, when we can learn to release our own pain and exchange our pain for the promises of Yah/God, to welcome the Healer to take this pain and reshape our hearts and minds, we can obtain rest. I want you to be honest because, in life, we can be great at burying the things that hurt us and the people we've hurt. We can put on a face that says everything is alright, hiding our true heart.

The truth is that we might be bitter toward those who have mistreated us. We have forgiven but did not forget how people treated us. We have shut doors in our lives because we are scared of what anyone else would do. We haven't stepped up to start a business because we are afraid we will fail.

We don't want to date again because the last marriage wasn't good, nor was the relationship before that. We are questioning our choices, regretting the past, and calling ourselves stupid. We are angry, we are mad at the circumstances, and we are taking the pain out on ourselves, our dreams, our hopes, our marriage, those that could love us, and limiting God.

Sometimes, the situation doesn't have to change; how we live and what we think needs to change. It's not always about how you feel but what you choose to believe. Journey with me... Let's go through these six areas to release pain from our lives and break any covenants we have made with evil powers that limit our lives.

It's time to Release Pain. I also invite you to the Immersive Experience, where you can journey through this powerful book with me, Dr. Krystal Lee. Scan the QR for my free reading plan, and enter the experience, which includes audio, videos, and my special gift!

Author K Lee

INTRODUCTION

RELEASE PAIN
ROBBERY

ROBBERY

I remember coming home. My side door was kicked in, the door to my garage was opened, and my dog was running out to greet me. I was nervous at first about entering, but nothing seemed to give the impression that the thief or thieves were still there. I didn't walk in but called the police.

I waited for the officer for about ten minutes or so. He checked out the place for me and told me it was all clear. I told my children to stay in the car. I went into the house unalarmed because I knew I had no valuables really worth stealing in my house. I had no tvs, no game systems, tablets, computers, or fancy clothes that immediately came to mind.

If a thief broke in, he might be disappointed because nothing was there. I am glad we weren't there, too. Sometimes, we are called away by God when others intend to harm us. We could get mad for coming home to a robbed home, or we could get thankful that we weren't there and didn't have to deal with the fallout of being home.

I thought nothing was missing, and I told the cop that when he drew up his report. He did make a note in his report about the side door, interior door, and related damage. I was glad because I didn't want the landlord to blame me for anything.

RELEASE PAIN

The owner had a side door to the garage they did not repair when I moved in. They put up a piece of plywood on the inside of the garage to block the entrance, but the door was never properly secured until after the break-in.

The locks on the garage door were not deadbolts either, and the door was not a security door but an interior door that they thought would be sufficient. The thief quickly must have kicked the door open, messing up the doorjamb. Now, they had to do the repairs I had already asked for in light of the break-in.

I didn't realize until the police left that they had stolen my two cameras, which were in a bag in my closet. I wasn't mad about the cameras, but the footage. I wanted what was on the cards. I had filmed many sermons from my mother, and I wanted to edit and upload them for her. I never got the chance.

It sucks when people take stuff you had plans for. Having your sense of security taken from you can equally suck. I didn't have a deep-seated fear of being at home after, but I can understand if others feel a strong sense of being violated knowing someone rummaged through their things. My reaction to the break-in was simple. I needed to get an alarm system because my shih tzu wasn't scaring anyone, lol.

Not everyone has my light-hearted approach to being robbed in this instance. A close friend of mine and his wife were away on their honeymoon. After those four or five days, they came home to find everything that they had shared together was gone. The intruder came through a window in their bottom-level apartment.

They did have valuables like game systems,

ROBBERY

TVs, and other expensive items a person could sell or pawn, I guess. His wife was so uncomfortable staying in the home that she made both of them relocate to live with her parents. Feeling this loss and experiencing someone take what was hers sent her into fear of living alone and, worse, with her husband.

She could no longer live alone, and even after the two of them separated and parted ways years later, she was still living with her parents. She was stuck in a moment, and she didn't feel safe in her marriage because she was uncertain and fearful after being robbed. She was robbed in more than one way. She lost her things, but she also lost her belief in her husband and his ability to keep her safe. She blamed him or allowed the event to play into her hidden fears of him not being able to provide or protect her.

She felt safer at home with her parents than in this very recent marriage. This seemingly simple matter caused a plethora of problems in their relationship. Her lack of confidence in him led to his uncertainty and probably underlined his insecurity about what he had accomplished so far in life.

Her parents believed he did not have what it took to be a husband to their daughter. They wanted to see him take a path that wasn't his. He wanted to be an actor, but instead, he eventually studied and graduated to drive trucks. This, too, was beneath their preference, and it didn't help that they stayed back at their house. This close family circle made it difficult for him to be a husband to her and for them to have a private relationship. It was subject to other people's scrutiny.

He felt that he missed out on having a wife, and she felt that she missed out on having a provider. Sometimes, we marry people for the right reasons but at the wrong time and for reasons that are not our priorities. The two of them got along well, played games and sports, could talk about anything that was funny, and shared a connection.

But when it came to raising children, paying bills, earning money, and determining where and how they would live, they were not on the same page. They each had a plan for their lives, but if they were honest, neither one of them talked enough about the issues that would rob them of their fantasy of having a marriage and happily ever after.

Sometimes, the biggest thief is not the one who will kick your door in but those who kill a dream or abide by a false truth—those who will tell you what you cannot have or what you are not. I remember once watching this video on TikTok of a man and woman having to match the color of bottles on a table. Beneath the table were the colored bottles they were to line up to match in the same order. Whenever they had one positioned right or how many, they would call out the number that was correct. They essentially had to shuffle the colors around when the number of correct ones decreased.

Many times, the man was getting the bottles in the right place, and the woman refused to allow him to be right even though when she moved the bottles around, she would hear "0 correct." Instead of listening and considering his opinions, she got mad at him and told him not to touch the ones she had wrong.

He was in a tight place and kept trying to move the other bottles to align. After she was exhausted from hearing "0" every time she moved her bottles around, he had to move quickly to set things correctly. Once he got it right after her objection for each bottle, they heard "5 correct." She shrugged

ROBBERY

her shoulders and said it didn't make sense.

Have you ever been under a person's thumb who kept you from making the right decisions? People who have taken from you the choices you wanted and needed to make? People who broke into places they did not belong, limiting your comfort and shoving you into a box?

The Bible says that the devil is a thief, seeking to kill, steal, and destroy (John 10:10). He is not happy when you are happy. He loves messy relationships, complications, churches that don't live up to the word of God, and how people can use your comforts against you. Most people who think of robbing you study your behaviors.

They want to know when you are home and away. If they think to steal your car or kidnap you in a parking lot, they watch you as you shop, come out of the store, and attempt to put your groceries up. A key deterrent to thieves is for you to be alert and vocal. It is easy to rob people who are unaware of the danger. I know it could be so unfair to feel you have to live your life on high alert.

High alert is different from alert. Being aware is different from being paranoid. To be aware is to be considerate of your surroundings. As a cop or soldier, it can become second nature to find the exit signs when you enter a room. My dad does it as second nature. A thief also does the same thing if they are scoping out a bank. They are looking for cameras, where people stand, tellers, and where the safes are located. They are scoping the place to plan their attack.

For many people who have been around you, when the one who steals from you is a friend or a family member, it is the worst kind of violation. You question if you have been too nice. Too open, too kind, or too understanding. Some of us have brought people into our homes to help them in a jam, and it is these people who steal from us.

I remember that a family friend told me when she was in the hospital, she sent people to her house to help her clean while she was away. These people, who were friends, said they wanted to help her. Turned out they were only looking for an opportunity to barge into her home when she was not there and take what they wouldn't dare take in her presence.

When she arrived home from the hospital, her house wasn't cleaned, and the items she was expecting to see were gone! She called them to ask them about them, and they said, "I didn't think you would need them." So, were they planning on her death? Or for her not to notice they robbed her?

The heartbreak that can settle in when people take from you when you are not expecting it can be crushing. When you are down, for them to take from you and act so heartless when asked about it can make you adjust your character. It can make you want to solve your own problems and not trust anyone after.

This is what the enemy is banking on. Evil spirits are waiting for an idle word you speak to be manifested in a covenant and agreement for them to be activated. Evil spirits need words to gain permission to operate in this world. When they lost their bodies back in the flood, they now have to live through the words of people. They need you to send them to do things and utilize their gifts and abilities to inflict pain on others.

When you get to a point where you want to take vengeance yourself, you are a prime candidate for the enemy and kingdom of darkness to use you.

ROBBERY

I know we may think I am not activating an evil spirit just because I don't want to live in my house, and I leave. But do you not see that fear has crept up and taken your security?

You might say this man was no good anyway. I should have never married him. But who told you to marry him in the first place? If so many things were wrong, what made you confident in marrying? What was speaking then that is not speaking now? I am not arguing about whether the marriage should have survived or not; it is not my place, but sometimes, we make life-long decisions based on facts that could easily change.

Getting married because you are pregnant might sound good at the time. But what if the pregnancy wasn't supposed to happen? A drunken night could mean pregnancy can come when uninvited. You might think about covering one sin, believing that covering it will keep you from experiencing any backlash later.

Trying to cover the sin and getting married didn't delay what this couple already knew: they weren't compatible. The baby that was the core reason for them saying "I do" died two weeks to the day of the marriage. To have been robbed physically, then robbed by losing a baby, and then to lose the marriage is a lot of loss. It can bring a cloud over your head that only Yah could remove.

It can make you feel things no one else can fathom. Losing a baby is hard. I remember coming to the wedding and, several weeks later, coming to the funeral. Nothing was more difficult than seeing a baby coffin. We don't know what Yah's plans are, but we must trust Him to work all things for our good. When we speak words that we don't think will land, be careful. One of the parents said, "I don't want this baby. I want to be married for a few years before the baby. I don't want to get married now but in a year."

Repeatedly, he said this but went along with the marriage. I remember saying, "Be careful what you say. Every word we say can live–can bring life or death." When you are on the job and constantly complaining about hatting it and not liking your manager, wanting to be somewhere else, or desiring for this to be your last day. When that word is manifested, why do we panic?

We can rob ourselves with our words. Spirits who have an ear to the ground could move on what you say out of frustration. We say things quickly, thinking we are having a friendly conversation. "Every time I get ahead, here something comes. It's like I keep going up to go down."

When we speak like this, we can think we are just being honest with ourselves. However, we can be the main reason we feel robbed. We may say, how can we rob ourselves? We can talk ourselves out of the moves we should make. We can allow a person in our lives to keep rearranging our choices to their liking. Even though we know it is wrong, we can be quiet to please them.

We are landing "0" points, growing frustrated, and eventually, we have to ignore them and move on our gut and confirmed movements. Why do we allow people who don't have the right order to move us backward? They are not helping us move forward but pulling us back. We think this is normal, but this is not the intention of healthy relationships. Yes, sometimes people won't agree, and sometimes you will make mistakes, but if you are trying to walk with someone, how if you both don't agree?

I remember saying a quick prayer when

ROBBERY

I finished watching the video, "I pray he doesn't marry a woman like this." When we marry people who are not in agreement with "anything" we want to do, it is founded on a weak foundation that is easily broken. You don't want to build your pillars in life on weak foundations. How you see yourself shouldn't be based on people who don't know you. People who haven't amassed for themselves what you want in life, shouldn't carry much weight either.

We can feel pain when we are robbed physically, and things are taken from us. When the life we should have lived is taken in a moment, many are thrown off for how to go forward. People who we trust can let us down, but if we don't allow anyone in, including God, we won't have the blessing of restoration. We won't see Him as healer, protector, and provider.

We have to forgive those who have taken from us and left us empty-handed. We must forgive ourselves so we can allow God to rebuild what was damaged. When we forgive others, we still have to release the pain from the violation. We have to give our vengeance to Yah. We have to trust Him to reset the right heart in us. It is not easy to release the pain that is buried deep.

If you want to easily release pain, you have to become more consistent in prayer. You have to give any case of robbery to Yah immediately. You don't want to delay. When we hesitate to give things to Him and allow our hearts to be entangled in injustice, we can lean on options that will limit us physically, spiritually, or psychologically. You want to be free, as Natalie Nichole writes in her second book, "I Will Be Free."

The way to be free is to release pain. Release the pain you have felt for years, or you feel now, by exposing your true issue with others to God. You are not complaining as you begin to share with Him. You are releasing your heart from pinned-up emotions. It can take time to get it all out, and there might be other issues mentioned in this book that have you bound; we will address that, too.

Right now, I want you to continue to reflect on the verses sprinkled in this chapter that will help you work through robbery. Each verse is positioned to help build you up and point to what is wrong. It is wrong to steal. Two verses that point to stealing being wrong are Deuteronomy 5:19, "'And you shall not steal," and Exodus 20:15, "You shall not steal."

These verses point to stealing being wrong and against God's commands. It is better to ask than to steal, and asking could mean praying for the means to earn it or to handle being without. It is not about it being a New Testament or Old Testament thing; it is about truth. We are not to steal because we don't know the pain we will cause by taking what belongs to someone else.

Then there are those who know what it costs and will steal from you anyway. Those who know how taking something will impact someone else and they don't care. They plan out their crimes and think to cover it up. King David knew the crime he

ROBBERY

was committing, but he didn't pump the breaks. He planned a kidnapping and determined to take a man's wife, and against her will.

When King David robbed Uriah and Bathsheba, he had to pay for that. He couldn't pray off the judgment. When he stole a man's wife and then put him on the front lines to die, it was determined that the consequence was him losing the life of his son. It broke Uriah's wife's heart, Bathsheba. She was innocent, and so was the baby. She didn't count it robbery for the Lord to take their son, though. She knew that the good Lord gives and takes away. She didn't run away from Yah because of her loss. She didn't hate Him for it.

She prayed to see His mighty hand in her situation. She wanted to be redeemed. She wanted her life back. The truth, her life wasn't ever the same, but Yah took a moment of rape, kidnapping, and losing her husband, all tricks of the enemy to rob her, and turned it to her GOOD! She was the only woman who bore a child that the Father used to build His Kingdom from David.

The Good Lord made her son, King Solomon, wise and the richest man on earth. Sometimes, our good news comes after someone has robbed us. Sometimes, after we feel great loss, that is when the Father fills the gap with something greater. It was not Yah's will for King David to kidnap and rape Bathsheba. That was a sin of King David. People who have stolen from you were not planned by God, but He can turn it to be for your Good!

No good thing will he keep from you (Psalm 84:11)! Read the verses in this chapter and let them encourage you. Allow them to nurture your soul and remind you that your greater is coming, and in fact, it is already here!

We serve a God above time who can redeem what was lost. He can give you back what the enemy stole through people, ill-treatment, and any place the thief broke in and took something. Keep journeying with me and see and experience the Good News! But also, heed the warnings.

When the thief is not someone else, it could be you. We talked about robbing yourself, but can we be guilty of robbing God? Malachi 3:8 says, "Will a man rob God? Yet you are robbing me. But you say, 'How have we robbed you?' In your tithes and contributions." This is a favorite for calling for tithes and offerings in the church. But when you read this entire chapter, you get the context.

We rob Yah when we don't give to the house of God because it keeps the church weak to perform what the Father wants to use money and resources to do. He has given the church, the Body of Christ, gifts and talents, a lifestyle He expects us to live. We live holy and support the church because it is Yah's instrument, a place to work miracles and gather the lost.

He says, beginning in verse 1 of Malachi 3:

"Behold, I send my messenger, and he will prepare the way before me. And the Lord whom you seek will suddenly come to his temple; and the messenger of the covenant in whom you delight, behold, he is coming, says the Lord of hosts.

2 But who can endure the day of his coming, and who can stand when he appears? For he is like a refiner's fire and like fullers' soap.

3 He will sit as a refiner and purifier of silver, and he will purify the sons of Levi and refine them like gold and silver, and they will bring offerings in righteousness to the Lord.

ROBBERY

4 Then the offering of Judah and Jerusalem will be pleasing to the Lord as in the days of old and as in former years.

5 Then I will draw near to you for judgment. I will be a swift witness against the sorcerers, against the adulterers, against those who swear falsely, against those who oppress the hired worker in his wages, the widow and the fatherless, against those who thrust aside the sojourner, and do not fear me, says the Lord of hosts."

It can be tempting to look at what is taking place and think there is no law, that nothing will happen to those who violate you, or that nothing will happen to the thief in our time. How many criminals go free and never to be found? What do we do when what is right seems to go unchecked?

Here, the Father is saying He is looking at how we live. He will refine us like silver and gold, pulling out the impurities found in us. Yes, it is possible to be a victim, and the Father seeks to show us something in our struggle. But the good news is that the Father is the one who will judge against those who are practicing manipulation and plotting your robbery. Those who saw that you were new to the neighborhood and threw you aside like the sojourner.

Proverbs 29:24 says: "The partner of a thief hates his own life; he hears the curse but discloses nothing." Those who swore they saw nothing and did, there is a clapback for that. Those who are kept silent will be the ones who will share in the judgment. I know you know the ones who know what happened and could help answer your questions, but they don't. Don't worry, the Father has eyes that don't close. He is all-knowing and all-powerful.

Like how the young lady went to her parents for security, Yah is the greatest Father we could ever have. He is concerned and cares for you. He will cover and restore to us what was taken. For some of us, what was taken was not a thing. It was not something that was external but something internal. For those of us who have lost time in any capacity, I want to encourage you.

When those we love are gone, it can leave a deep hole in our hearts that is not easily filled. If we try to fill it with drinks, relationships, sex, food, or sleep, nothing will fill this gap in our hearts. We must allow the presence of Yah to come in and restore us. He says in John 10:10, "The thief comes only to steal and kill and destroy. I came that they may have life and have it abundantly.."

For some of us, when death came, it killed a parent, grandparent, child, husband, wife, or someone we loved and cared about. It took from us and robbed us of time with them. We cannot get them back, and the plans that were to happen are now thwarted in our hearts and minds. We are now walking aimlessly, or we stopped yearning for what was before because we don't see a way forward.

I remember when my niece passed away. My sixteen-year-old niece wanted to leave, and she did because of complications with diabetes. This was the hardest death I have had to endure to date. I know it was harder for her mother, my older sister. But it was a hard blow to the family. We all prayed and trusted that Yah would give more. We trusted that the truths others could report for coming back from the dead could be her story.

She had two heart attacks in close proximity. One made her unconscious, but she was still breathing. The second one, she couldn't breathe for a longer period, and she needed life support eventually to regulate her breathing. When we got the

ROBBERY

news that she was brain-dead and would ultimately die, my family began to pray harder. My sister and I prayed over her, and we couldn't easily accept that this would be the last time we would touch her hand, touch her feet, feel her face. With tears running from our faces, we prayed over her.

We were willing not to see this as robbery but as a way for her to release the pain she was held in for sixteen years. She was in pain, and we couldn't stop it. She stopped taking her medicine for many years. She wouldn't take it because she wanted to be healed or to die. She made some poor choices socially, but the pain she felt was manifesting in other ways, and she was looking for rest.

She wanted something the world could not give her. She was unsatisfied with the doctor's words. She sought to take things into her own hands by her choices. She was harsh to her mother, but not once did her mother give up on her. Not once did she accept that her daughter was doomed to die because of this deadly disease. She prayed for better news.

What if the better news feels like robbery to one or many? She was young, but her battle started at age 3. She never liked being sick. She was near death many times. She would come out of the hospital and fight to smile. To build up a desire to be here and not somewhere else. We couldn't remove the pain she felt here, but Yah could remove it where she is.

We saw a miracle in the hospital that day. A person who wasn't supposed to move moved several times. The one who we thought wouldn't have last words spoke from a hospital bed with no words. She told us through the spirit that she was fine and had released pain. Her mother had already forgiven her of many things, but she needed to release her from being here. It is never easy to see a child buried; that was the first funeral I participated in from the service standpoint. The first time, I was a chaplain in the hospital working with the family–and it was my family!

Even as I write this book, tears fall from my eyes, and I have to search my heart for how to honor all that I want to do for her. I went to the steak dinner I had promised her in honor of her. I did allow her to drive my van, which was scary at the time, but I am glad I did it. I am writing a novel in her dedication, "What If," and I am excited about how it will help share a different perspective on life and death.

Exodus 20:12: "Honor your father and your mother, that your days may be long in the land that the Lord your God is giving you." We are to honor our parents so that our days will be long here on the earth. When we are not, it can cut down on the time we have on earth. Not everyone's story is Syeda's. Some, it is because of how they have treated their parents.

If we are treating our parents poorly, we are robbing our time here on earth. Like in Malachi, how we treat people matters, and God is swift to judge it. When those around you are going through, be mindful of how you respond to the poor in spirit. To those who are struggling financially. To steal from those who are stretching out their hands for

ROBBERY

help is wrong.

Proverbs 22:22-23 reads, "Do not rob the poor, because he is poor, or crush the afflicted at the gate, 23 for the Lord will plead their cause and rob of life those who rob them." For the people who thought they were getting over by robbing my close friend, they must be careful and repent. Those who are taken from others should also take heed and know that stealing, especially from God's anointed, is not a good idea. When we steal from the poor or the weak, God will judge those actions. Nothing goes unnoticed by Him.

He doesn't have to make you give back what you stole. He can allow you to keep it like Judas. He sold the Messiah for thirty pieces of silver (Matthew 26:15). It wasn't until after that he realized the grave mistake he made because of greed. He allowed his greed to rob humanity of more time with the Messiah. He robbed himself of peace because peace is not reserved for the wicked (Isaiah 48:22). The scripture says, "There is no peace," says the Lord, "for the wicked."

We don't glory that others suffer because of a judgment of God because we all stand in the need of grace and mercy. We pray for those who have stolen from us, sincerely. These are the commandments of believers. Luke 6:28 says, "...bless those who curse you; pray for those who abuse you."

How can we pray for those who have robbed us, abused us, or even cursed us? We have to remember where to place our eyes and heart. Some of us have learned to steal not because we like it but out of necessity. What do you do when you have to feed your family, and you don't have it? Some may think that because they got away with it once before, God might be okay with it as a lifestyle.

RELEASE PAIN

A close family member of mine had a run end with stealing many times. When he was younger, he did it with his friends and got juvenile. He served his time, but I dare say he didn't learn the lesson. When he got older, he thought about doing the same thing. He didn't have a gun, but that person did. So, it became an armed robbery.

His charge and severity were not as much because he was younger than the other guy, but he got more time than the last time. He understood the punishment but complained about it because he thought his sentence was too long based on his part in the crime. It took him two sentences to learn to stop stealing.

Serving time is the courts' way of punishing you for a crime, but what about what the Father feels you need to do or repay? He missed out on time with his children. He missed out on being with the wife of his youth. He missed out on living the life he could have. His age trickled up, and now restarting, life is not so easy as a felon.

Unlike before, getting his own place and getting on his feet proved to be harder. The hardship, the rejection, and the complications made him turn to drugs to cope. What he thought he got by breaking in to steal, he lost so much more. Ephesians 4:28 says, "Let the thief no longer steal, but rather let him labor, doing honest work with his own hands, so that he may have something to share with anyone in need."

He had to learn a lesson that will come to the forefront the longer we live on earth: quick money doesn't last long. You will learn the value of laboring for what you want and need. In the Garden, Adam was told he had to work by the sweat of his brow. Genesis 3:19 records, "By the sweat of your face you shall eat bread, till you return to the

ROBBERY

ground, for out of it you were taken; for you are dust, and to dust you shall return." Anyone thinking to do something different and go another way is attempting to rob God.

When we work, it may be tempting to base our effort on what we can buy. Those who steal usually steal things because they don't have them or enjoy the thrill of taking something for nothing. But you are obligated to repay anything you take. Stealing is an invisible commitment to the author of stealing, and that is not Yah.

If there are things you want, work for them. If you have been robbed of your things, don't get down. Remember not to store up your value in things that can deteriorate, rot, rust, and any good thief can take. Store up your values and treasures in heaven, where they will have lasting value.

Mathew 6:19-21 says, "Do not lay up for yourselves treasures on earth, where moth and rust destroy and where thieves break in and steal, 20 but lay up for yourselves treasures in heaven, where neither moth nor rust destroys and where thieves do not break in and steal. 21 For where your treasure is, there your heart will be also."

This does not mean you cannot have nice things or what you desire, but don't base your world on the value of an object or thing. Some people worship cars, jewelry, purses, and other things that matter to them. It is a scary day when you will rob one person to afford things. This is not about survival but about getting your desires by any means. This is not the right heart toward people, yourself, or God.

Sometimes, the thing we are chasing is not an object but a person. Again, storing up our treasure in a wife or husband doesn't always lead to the best outcomes. That same person you gave up your life for can turn on you and leave you empty. When we have our heart in Yah, it is a sure foundation. He will never leave nor forsake you.

Hebrews 13:5 says, Keep your life free from love of money, and be content with what you have, for He has said, "I will never leave you nor forsake you. It can be tempting to believe the love of money, and the safety of having money is better for you than Yah. We can think that having money can replace having Him in our lives, especially if we were robbed. We think that having more would help to prevent the sting if it comes again. It might, but losing your peace to chase after things stolen is never a good trade-off.

Lying to protect your interest in stealing is not right, also. We do not want to steal from others because we were robbed. When we become the thief, we don't make matters better but worse. As believers, we have to trust that Yah has a plan to bless us as we release the pain of being robbed. The evidence of releasing pain is not having the desire to steal, to deal falsely with others, or to lie to someone to get your way. Leviticus 19:11 says, "You shall not steal; you shall not deal falsely; you shall not lie to one another."

Our posture after being robbed is important so that we don't become bound. Release the Pain of being robbed, and you do that by accepting that where you are right now, God can change it. "He Can Do It for You!" Have you heard of that song, "Lord Do it for Me" by Zacardi Cortez? It is a powerful song that will help point you in the right direction as you pray on contentment for what you have and what you hope for, which you pursue through faith in action.

EMPOWERING SCRIPTURES: ROBBERY

Malachi 3:8 Will a man rob God? Yet you are robbing me. But you say, 'How have we robbed you?' In your tithes and contributions.
John 10:10 - The thief comes only to steal and kill and destroy. I came that they may have life and have it abundantly.

Hebrews 13:5 Keep your life free from the love of money, and be content with what you have, for he has said, "I will never leave you nor forsake you

Genesis 3:19 By the sweat of your face you shall eat bread, till you return to the ground, for out of it you were taken; for you are dust, and to dust you shall return

Ephesians 4:28 Let the thief no longer steal, but rather let him labor, doing honest work with his own hands, so that he may have something to share with anyone in need.

Leviticus 19:11 You shall not steal; you shall

not deal falsely; you shall not lie to one another.

Deuteronomy 5:19 And you shall not steal.

Exodus 20:15 You shall not steal.

Joel 2:25 I will restore to you the years that the swarming locust has eaten, the hopper, the destroyer, and the cutter, my great army, which I sent among you.

Proverbs 29:24 The partner of a thief hates his own life; he hears the curse but discloses nothing.

Proverbs 22:23 for the Lord will plead their cause and rob of life those who rob them.

Mathew 6:19-21 Do not lay up for yourselves treasures on earth, where moth and rust[a] destroy and where thieves break in and steal, 20 but lay up for yourselves treasures in heaven, where neither moth nor rust destroys and where thieves do not break in and steal. 21 For where your treasure is, there your heart will be also.

Isaiah 48:22 There is no peace, says the Lord, "for the wicked."

Matthew 26:15 and said, "What will you give me if I deliver him over to you?" And they paid him thirty pieces of silver.

Habakkuk 2:6-8 Shall not all these take up their taunt against him, with scoffing and riddles for him, and say, "Woe to him who heaps up what is not his own—for how long?—and loads himself with pledges!" 7 Will not your debtors suddenly arise, and those awake who will make you tremble? Then you will be spoiled for them. 8 Because you have plundered many nations, all the remnant of the peoples shall plunder you, for the blood of man and violence to the earth, to cities and all who dwell in them.

1 Peter 5:7 casting all your anxieties on him because he cares for you.

Romans 9:18 So then he has mercy on whomever he wills, and he hardens whomever he wills.

YOUR POWER AND FOUNDATION

Again Habakkuk 2:6-8 says, "Shall not all these take up their taunt against him, with scoffing and riddles for him, and say, "Woe to him who heaps up what is not his own—for how long?—and loads himself with pledges!" 7 Will not your debtors suddenly arise, and those awake who will make you tremble? Then you will be spoiled for them. 8 Because you have plundered many nations, all the remnant of the peoples shall plunder you, for the blood of man and violence to the earth, to cities and all who dwell in them."

For those who are guilty of taking from you, you must know and believe there is a consequence. No, that punishment doesn't have to come at your hand or at your preferred time. Those who are doing terrible things, breaking into people's homes, stealing from family members, or committing other acts, there is a penalty.

The God we serve says to cast those cares on Him (1 Peter 5:7), and He will deal with them, showing mercy how He chooses to have mercy (Romans 9:18). We don't get to dictate mercy, nor do we determine a punishment. Our job is to remain blameless. How can we rob someone else of the blessing of forgiveness because we feel they don't deserve it?

Be encouraged that what was taken from you, God is able to repay and give you more than you ever asked for. If you lose a child, a spouse, a job, a house, or a future, He is able to give you something that will make the loss appear to be part of His big plan. His plan is always for you to win– no matter what befalls you.

Don't think there is a trick the devil can perform, or a friend or foe, to thwart the Father's plans to hold you in His arms. Don't believe for a second that He will not repair what was broken and set your life on a path that will be victorious!

I know today might feel heavy, but read these verses that remind you He has not forgotten about those who have stolen from you. Companies that robbed you, family, friends, spouses, and even your children. He is faithful to repay and show mercy, giving grace as we all need to those whom He chooses.

As you work to release the pain that was married to fear, rejection, frustration, and bitterness, allow Him to reset your mind and heart today. Allow Him to encourage your spirit and remind you of His goodness. Naomi, in the bible, lost her husband and two sons. When she thought she had nothing to live for, Yah had plans to turn it around!

How was she going to have grandchildren, God promised, with no sons? She had no husband to make more, and even if she could, she would be

ROBBERY

so old by the time they were grown. She felt a heavy burden. But the Father did something she never suspected.

He gave her double for her trouble! The enemy thought to wipe her out an steal her legacy with her sons' deaths. Yet, God gave her Ruth to restart her legacy! Ruth went to marry Boaz, gave her a grandson, and she became the grandmother of King David! I know it can look bleak when we are standing on the battleground during war. The battle could look like we lost when those we love have been taken.

Be encouraged, my sister or even my brother. We win this battle, and we win not by robbing or taking out vengeance that is fueled by anger and evil thoughts. We win by allowing our Father to heal our hearts. Rejuvenating our will to do right by others so we can stand in right standing with Him. It is not about being weak but showing ourselves strong in faith. We have to take the high road even when we have nothing telling us to do that.

The enemy wants you to crap out and have nothing. But GOD! said, "Not So. It is Not Finished!" I want you to listen to a song by Maurette Brown Clark that got me through called "It Ain't Over." The line I love is that she says, "It ain't over until God says it's done! No, no, no, no, no..."

RELEASE PAIN

What power and encouragement is in that song! Raise your spirits and hope today. Shalom, sister or brother, let's keep moving forward.

ROBBERY

INJUSTICE

No one likes being played, do we? We all have a strong dislike for when someone is trying to get over on us. Even if we allow it, we are not happy about it. It doesn't mean we don't see it because we often do. There are several factors that injustice plays a hand in that make our skin boil, and we pump the breaks on what we need to do.

I know we might think, why should injustice make it into a book like this? We are more than the people we date and the family we are born to. We have dreams and aspirations, and for many of us, we thought justice would prevail, right? We thought justice would be on the side of truth.

I can tell you that I have been bitter before because I did not like how I was treated by people, companies, organizations, elections, and the list could go on. I remember when I purchased a house at a time in my life when money was a bit tight. I got this house as a fixer-upper, and it was in good enough condition to have a traditional house insurance policy and not a rehab policy.

I took out a loan for 20k to renovate the house and things seemed to be going well until it wasn't. I hired a company that did not get the work done, and the work they started was also poorly done. I hired another contractor to fix their mistakes. I lost about 7k in this fiasco. To make matters worse, the contractor filed for bankruptcy, and although I was added to the list of debtors, I knew I would never see my refund. It has been eleven years, and I haven't gotten a dime!

Going to that court was frustrating because even though I won the case, I did not get the prize. I was on the right side of justice. This company was hired to tear down my three-story deck, which was pulling the house down. It wasn't properly supported to begin with, so the deck needed to be removed. As they tour down the deck, however, they snatched out parts of siding, and you could see daylight through the doors they should have sealed off. It was a mess.

The side porch they were also paid to create, the posts were inserted wrong, the cement was wrong, and the driveway was trash because of how they discarded debris. I had rock cement all throughout the backyard they did not clean up, and they pulled the dumpster before I could get it up.

At this time, I was 125 pounds, so lifting heavy cement blocks was not something I could do for prolonged periods. I had to keep moving with my project even though I didn't have the work I paid for or the money I was owed. The court system did nothing to ensure I got my money, but those who were to be paid before me, like his cars and house, were promised first dibs, and the money he was using to pay them was my money!

I was heartbroken because of this house. But I wasn't completely deflated. The next contractor I hired was the plumber. He was to re-plumb the house because the pipes were old. He did not know what he was doing, although he was licensed. His insurance paperwork was a farce. He did not have

INJUSTICE

adequate insurance, so the work he did for a few thousand dollars also had to be fixed.

In two contracts, I lost 10k. On top of that, I had to pay for the electrical to be redone because the wires going into the box did not pass code. These were all simple things, and nothing was major, but having to re-borrow 20k to fix the errors was no longer part of the budget. The second plumber I hired was amazing. I wished I had known him sooner.

He told me how he also got burned working in construction. He accepted a job where he was fixing another company's work. Because he was the listed contractor at the time of the inspections, he was nailed with all of the issues. He was sued by the client and blamed for everything.

He not only lost what they paid him, but he also had to pay about 100k out of his own pocket to cover damages that exceeded his one million dollar bond. He taught me a valuable lesson but also created incredible fear. I know a lot of people tell you to buy a fixer-upper, but they can underestimate what they can cost if you hire the wrong people.

If you get robbed and the courts can't help you. Needless to say, running out of money was my worst nightmare or a repair that would blow my budget all the same. I had one more major issue that crept up: mold.

Surprisingly, I survived getting the plumbing fixed and the electricity done right the first time. My electrician was the best! Now, I am at a hurdle. I was running out of money, and I was nearly done. The rest was mostly cosmetics like bathrooms and fixing the kitchen cabinets and counters I had already bought.

RELEASE PAIN

I bought the appliances, counters, and windows. I scraped popcorn off ceilings to make my vision happen. I was passing the inspections, too. I was happy until I found the mold. There was a leak upstairs that happened from the weather or something like that. I had an adjuster come out to tell me the loss was not covered in full. They issued a $700 estimate on the loss of my things but did not compensate me for anything else that was effected, and of course, my deductible was $1,000.

I thought about how everything I lost could not be covered or even how $20,000 in personal coverage could be reduced to $700 in value! The water from the pipe overflowed and soaked all of my items. I had tons of clothes I had to toss. I had a Mac laptop computer and other electronics that were useless. I thought I would report them to the Bureau of Insurance, but I didn't understand the process back then.

At that moment, I lost everything. I couldn't keep re-fixing, and I couldn't get the house refinanced. This was the nail in the coffin not to get an insurance payout that was owed to me. This isn't the first time an insurance company didn't pay out what they were supposed to.

I remember I lived with my sister briefly in a bottom-unit apartment. On this particular night, it was raining heavily. I mean, it rained for two or three days straight. The gutters in the apartment complex were not flushed out well, so the water started to back up into the patio areas of some downstairs units. The water started to trickle in and then it wouldn't stop. When we woke up and saw downstairs, it was about 2 feet of water. Couches were stained, tvs stopped working, and toys and other items were completely ruined that sat on the floor.

INJUSTICE

It was in the lease agreement you had to have renters insurance. My sister thought, thank God I paid for that. She called the company, and they said it was not a covered loss because it was an act of God. She told them it wasn't. The issue was clogged gutters that backed up only her unit. The rest of the complex was fine, but our building was not.

They said in that case, it would be on the apartment complex to cover her damages. She promptly phoned them, and they said the same thing. It was not their fault but renters insurance because things like this could happen. Needless to say, my sister lost all of her property in that flood and never got a dime from either party.

She looks at insurance differently because of that, and I did, too. For those of us who have been burned by insurance, we tend to avoid them unless we are required to have them. Then we don't expect them to pay unless we are not at fault because if we are at fault, we know already what will happen. They love collecting payments each month, but we all know that the moment you have a claim, your bill will skyrocket, or you will be dropped like a hot potato with no remorse. Then, to make it worse, if you try to go elsewhere, they will penalize you for a claim you made with another company!

We think, how is this legal? How is it fair to have people pay into policies that they pray they never need to use? Something is very wrong with this, and it seems very unfair. Scenarios like this made me lose any confidence in insurance. I never thought about getting a policy of any kind after that house. I even didn't want to get back into home-ownership because I saw it as a money pit.

We don't have to look far to see the injustice of "black people" in America. We have been the victims of redlining and traps to steal our properties. We buy high and sell low, which seems to be the cycle that repeats in our neighborhoods. Who wouldn't be bitter toward homeownership when so many loopholes exist to take our homes for pennies on the dollar?

Job 5:16 says, "So the poor have hope, and injustice shuts her mouth." Have you ever thought that when you involve the courts in your matter, things will get better? The Bible tells us that if we have an issue with someone, we should try to settle it before going to court. The outcomes are not always fair, and with an unjust judge or jury and even poor circumstances, the outcomes can be crushing (Luke 12:57-59).

"And why do you not judge for yourselves what is right? 58 As you go with your accuser before the magistrate, make an effort to settle with him on the way, lest he drags you to the judge, and the judge hands you over to the officer, and the officer puts you in prison. 59 I tell you, you will never get out until you have paid the very last penny."

Sometimes, even when we are right, the burden of proof falls on us. I had a friend once who had to go to court for an insurance matter. You would think, okay, maybe property insurance is a roll of the dice, but what if your life insurance turns for the worse?

Many families think to provide something for their children or at least cover the cost of their burial. They think I should help remove this burden from my children and try to leave them something. There is usually one person to whom you hand the money to manage the spending. It doesn't necessarily mean this person was loved more or is a favorite.

INJUSTICE

But how many family members question the decision of the dead to pick who they did? They wonder, why not me? The injustice they might feel to be overlooked and not selected in such an important decision can sow discord between brethren or family. How many families have you seen fighting with each other on the days that they should be coming together to be there for each other?

People are fighting about furniture and maliciously holding something from another to inflict pain because they can. These people may use their power of influence with the family or finances to fight a decision they disagree with. Micah 2:1-2 describes their heart and intentions, "Woe to those who devise wickedness and work evil on their beds! When the morning dawns, they perform it because it is in the power of their hand. 2 They covet fields and seize them, and houses, and take them away; they oppress a man and his house, a man and his inheritance."

No matter what you say to defend the deceased decision, they see it as you trying to usurp your authority over them. It doesn't make them back down but riles them up. They put a target on your back and turn against you at a time when you need their help or love. They fight you on the funeral plans. They push to vote on decisions within the family about terms you were asked to resolve.

When the family cannot agree, and you must decide, they plant ideas in people's heads that this was your plan all along, to leave everyone with nothing and take everything. They say you want to control everything and leave everyone else with nothing, but you know that is not true. This was not your heart, but you have to make decisions as best as you can. Then, for what was left to you specifically, are you not entitled to keep?

RELEASE PAIN

Some feel what was left to you personally should be shared with the family. So, this difference in thought causes some families to go to court to fight over a will or life insurance policy. What should have brought assurance of love brought wrath and pain. When you should be hugging your child, uncle, mother, sister, brother, or parents, they stand as the plaintiff and you the defendant!

No matter the ruling, the ruling will change the family dynamics, and you try to deter that from happening. However, your attempts seem to be too small for the issue. You feel the injustice closing in around you as your uncle turns. He points to personal matters for why you are unfit to have the money. The sister with whom you shared a room tells you her children are equal to yours. Your brother says he could use the money more than you because you already have so much.

They join together and tell the judge how you are selfish. This battle goes on, and if the will isn't clear. If the policy is ambiguous or if there is an issue with any documentation. The materials for the deceased become subject to the judge. For them to rule on what happens to your property, 50% of your money disappears to the courts during probate!

Did your heart break when Chadwick Bosman died and he had no will? His wife and children needed that money, but the government has no problem with taking half as a penalty for poor planning. When families fight, the courts get a piece because you two couldn't agree. Family disputes and court rulings on money and the choices concerning those we love can be hard.

Those who lose can abandon the one who was standing in the right based on what was written by their shared loved one. They see the money as a divider and a privilege one has that makes them a

INJUSTICE

black sheep if they weren't before. Nothing is lonelier than going through the death of a loved one and then losing the rest of your family afterward.

I know of too many fights where physical fights ensued because of a legal dispute about money left to one family member and not the collective. I don't know why a parent would leave money for one child and not for the others. I don't know how people determine what they leave to who, but we don't have to understand it to accept it.

What I love about Yah is that whatever you need in life, He is able to supply your needs with or without what you think you must have. I know it is easy to hear but harder to believe. It can be hard to forgive our family who have abandoned us when we need them most. When you did nothing wrong, but you were challenged.

My mom, who is a licensed whole life agent selling insurance in Indiana and a few other states, told me how a person she talked to missed out on a policy from her husband. They were a young couple, so she was not hip to everything he bought. He died suddenly, and the only policy that was known was the one his parents helped him get.

There was enough in it to cover his burial and give the parents about 5k in cash. When the wife asked for some of the money, they told her, "James gave this money to us because he wanted us to have it." They gave her nothing. She was crying and scared because she had children with no means of providing for them that she and her husband shared.

She prayed and went home, not sure of what to do to make it to the next day. How many of you know God wasn't done? Any ill intent, hurtful prayers she thought to pray, it was good she didn't go there. Job 11:14 says, "If iniquity is in your hand, put it far away, and let not injustice dwell in your tents." We are to be holy because He says He is holy (1 Peter 1:16).

She kept living, and one day, she got a piece of mail. It was from an insurance company she was unaware of, and so she opened it because it was addressed to her. She thought that maybe God wanted her to get a policy, and this was a gentle reminder for her to get one for her children. She was the sole provider now, and she had no help.

She opened the letter, and it was a check for 100k. She went from not knowing what to do to make it to the next day rejoicing for how the Father made a way. He had multiple policies, and he never told anyone about them. He died, and with the circumstances, she was paid double his policy.

Proverbs 16:8 reads, "Better is a little with righteousness than great revenues with injustice." I am sure the parents felt some kind of way when she quoted the same in response. Isn't it like Yah to give you a lot with righteousness than the revenues of injustice? Sometimes, when we lose one battle, the Father will give us victory somewhere else. He knows how to provide.

The end might not be the end, although it feels like it. Injustice can break hope in us, can't it? When you need a win and you get a juicy "L," it

INJUSTICE

hurts, to say the least. The devil loves to push the button of injustice to get you angry and out of character so that you speak negatively about yourself. He wants you to cancel hopes for a future because of the current circumstances.

I have to admit, I used to be really big in politics when I was younger. When I was 18, I participated in donor events. I researched the details of both parties and weighed my decision. I wanted to be an "educated voter."

That year, things were awkward, to say the least, in Florida. I made my vote, and I watched the news explain how so many votes were not counted because they claimed the chad was dangling or not clear enough for them to count. They recounted, and recounted, but the results seemed rigged no matter what they said.

How does a system work so well, and then, all of a sudden, it breaks down and doesn't work for several precincts in counties that have a particular demographic of voters? The president at the time was a relative of the governing party in the state of Florida, which added more distrust of the system.

I didn't give up on voting altogether, but I lost the edge and excitement I had. The nail in the coffin, for me, was watching close races between candidates who I didn't like or believe in their integrity. When you hear people say confidently and matter-of-factly that you have to choose the lesser evil. I want to vomit in my mouth.

I couldn't celebrate either candidate, so choosing red or blue seemed like making the same choice. I voted for a while because of my ancestors and what it took to give us a voice. However, with the playing field so rigged, who could blame the many who battle on whether their vote really counts or if it will be counted?

It seems odd that you can win the popular vote but lose in electoral votes. The majority of the country could vote one way, and it takes a few key states to rule all of it as a non-issue. It is sobering to see people who appear to have good intentions looked over. Those who have taken bribes have even proven to have a sketchy background to rise to the top, which seems so unfair. It really makes you question your priorities and how you want to use your power of voting.

Election season is always a tough time for a country. No matter who wins or loses, there will always be those who disapprove of the outcome. Also, those who will try to steal votes and rig machines. Some will take to violence to release their frustration. Many claim they will relocate to another country, but very few ever do. Correct me if I am wrong. Why do we share our pain about the outcome of an election in ways that make us bitter or feel powerless?

What do we hope to change by giving up? The truth is if we don't change our response, our answer, the outcome will remain the same. I do believe there is a place for justice and the law. The law was given to judge lawbreakers (1 Timothy 1:9).

"Understanding this, that the law is not laid down for the just but for the lawless and disobedient, for the ungodly and sinners, for the unholy and profane, for those who strike their fathers and mothers, for murderers..."

For those who lost cases like this or saw the money and things split up, know that our Father doesn't like ugly. Jeremiah 22:13 records, "Woe to him who builds his house by unrighteousness, and his upper rooms by injustice, who makes his

INJUSTICE

neighbor serve him for nothing and does not give him his wages." It is a verse of comfort when you see how countries in the United Nations seem to be worse off now than before they joined.

The top five countries and the divide for wealth seemed to only deepen and then level out. I'm not sure if it was planned that way. I am no mathematician, but I do understand the frustration of leadership that says, why waste dollars on the UN membership when we get nothing more than a seat at the table and make the news? Could that money and time be better spent elsewhere? For some, that answer is yes and they are making decisions accordingly.

Seeing the injustice around the world with people, women, children, young men, or seniors is bothersome. No matter the continent, there are decisions being made that you question how can that be good for the people. Why would you want to tag all children at birth in Kenya?

What good can come from chipping children? Some may say nothing is wrong, but we see news articles that pop up and quickly disappear about how the "theys" of the world commit atrocious crimes against society, and no one judges them. How did we have a full-out worldwide pandemic that killed people all around the world, and no justice was brought forth on judging whatever happened to start it? How did the cause and placing blame disappear?

How are people who took the COVID-19 vaccine now on Aids medicine? I am no scientist, but a bate and switch is never an act of justice. Sneaking material into vaccines and not letting people know or guilt-tripping the world has to be wrong. Why should the whole world shut down and no one be held accountable? Is it true that this fabricated illness has no source? Or is the source too big, too important to fail?

Remember when banks were bailed out by President Obama? How many people lost their homes in the recession of the early 2000s when the housing bubble burst? Thousand upon thousands of homes went vacant after they purchased them at premiums. They were getting arm deals, fluctuating interest rates, and jumbo loans. The companies guilty of writing these policies were bailed out, and the people were told they were protected because they "were too big to fail."

Why not replace the corrupt companies and bring in ethical companies? Are the companies now better than before? Or do they have another scheme to play out on people in hopes that everyone will forget about the last one by that time? We can become skeptical when we experience injustice, can't we?

The banking system seems to be full of greed when you look at how compounding interest works. How do you pay five times what you bought a property for, and you can lose it by not paying taxes? How can you pay off the building but never own the land? If you pay off the house and don't pay taxes, or a claim of eminent domain is granted, you have no house, no land, nothing!

How can that be justice? How can you work to afford something when highrises go up across the street that make your small house unaffordable? Injustice looms in so many areas of our lives, doesn't it? How can we have peace, joy, and feel good when so many things are wrong?

We see the harm to the environment, animals, water, sky, and seas. How is it possible or legal to spray chemicals in the air and not give a

INJUSTICE

true PSA for what they are doing? If it is unlawful or dangerous to smoke around others, how are these particles safe, or better yet, what benefit do they provide? Why does the medical system seem to push us to drugs rather than to healing?

I know that during Covid, many families were complaining about healthcare. We were complaining because some death certificates were incorrect. Some people died from a heart attack, but their death certificate said Covid. We were denied access to check up on our relatives, so those who were battling cancer had to do it alone.

Can you imagine going through something already tough and then having to go it alone? I was pregnant with my youngest son during Covid. I gave birth to him in August of 2020. It was a quiet day. I was spending time at home, which was my preference even before Covid. I would get out to walk my dog and breathe in the air, and I would see a cute deer in the woods from time to time. I loved where I lived and the peace it gave me.

When the day arrived for me to give birth, I was excited to have my mother-in-law in the room. Up to that point, I had not taken a Covid test or had any issues with the virus. I was grateful that no one in my house got sick, either. We tried to keep clean and stay home, and with the grace of Yah, we were all healthy.

When I got to the hospital, they said only one person could be in the room. So I knew she would be the guest. Then they told me the terrible news. What they didn't tell me was that she could not come with me into the operating room "OR" unless I took a COVID test, not her but me! She could be with me in the labor and delivery area, and both of us not test, but not in the OR. I didn't have to test to go into the OR, but I couldn't have support with me.

I was crushed because, at the time, I wasn't sure why a virus needed to scrap the inner part of your throat through your nose. It seemed painful and suspicious. I have heard many stories and read history where medical outbreaks were not addressed in the same manner for all people. I knew about the Tuskegee project. Then the project that permitted lead paint to remain in complexes where black people and children lived. Then, the recent issues in Flint, Michigan, among other horror stories, were why I did not feel comfortable with testing.

I denied the test, and my mother-in-law understood, but I am sure she was sad. It was a moment I felt was unjust because how could a hospital make you wear a mask, see no signs, have no fever, and deny you your rights because of a blanket condition not relevant to you? Furthermore, if you had Covid, they would still deliver the baby all the same, so why should there be isolation? I understood it like we all did, but that doesn't mean we agreed with it.

That moment was taken from us, and to this day, I have had to learn to live with that moment of being alone, bringing my son into the world. Only I wasn't completely alone. Yah was in the room. It was also good that my doctor was the same for all of my children in Georgia, and so was the hospital, so I didn't feel too awkward about the situation. I remember joking and laughing as I stared away from the bright light hanging behind the blue drape. It wasn't a terrible time, but certainly not ideal.

I heard of how other hospitals didn't give out as much leniency as I had received, so I counted that blessing, too. I am not sure what the point of Covid was intended to be for the world. I don't know if it was meant to be a transfer of wealth like many have claimed. However, locking people inside and keeping them from working, events, restaurants, and places allowed a lot of us to slow down and analyze what was important to us.

For the many who were on auto-pilot, we had to wake from our sleep. I am sure a lot of money was made during Covid, but a lot of it was also swept away. Proverbs 13:23 says, "The fallow ground of the poor would yield much food, but it is swept away through injustice." The many who couldn't live a day without buying or shopping couldn't. The marriages that were on the brink came to a bubbling head during Covid. Conditions in the home either improved or waxed worse during Covid.

The way people spend money also changed during COVID-19. The way people work and desire to work has never been the same. There were job vacancies recently after Covid that some argue were not being filled or even applied for. Going to the Post Office in 2025, there are still complaints about staffing shortages. Some stores you frequented before can't keep staff even to this day. For people who couldn't get a job before, companies are throwing jobs and chances they wouldn't have before COVID-19; I'm not sure if this will be the pattern moving forward, but it is something to marvel at.

COVID-19 could have been meant for something terrible, and although bad things happened, some good was still able to poke through. Another occasion and testimony I must share is from a close relative of mine. She is talented and gifted in creative arts. She has always been meticulous with the things that can hold her attention.

She is dedicated, a hard worker, and not afraid to pay for what she wants to do. She has gone to more schools than me, and her studies have varied. She is equally interested in nail art and the medical field. She is smart in both fields, too. I saw her make the honor roll in both industries, and I tried my best to support her.

I hated that she got her degree from a technical program that charged her for a program they were not yet certified to offer. They were in the process of getting accredited, but they were running the program and making promises. In short, they didn't keep. When she was finishing up the program and graduating with honors, she was told she would get an update on their accreditation status in the mail.

She thought nothing of it and was excited to have finished the program. We celebrated her efforts, but the fanfare died down when we heard the news about the value of her education. Although she did the work, and the school became accredited about a month after her graduation, they refused to make prior students' graduation fall under the certification.

Not sure if this was an oversight or what happened, but she spent money and time on a medical assistant program that couldn't get her a job. She was frustrated, heartbroken, and thought to give up. My brother had a similar situation. He was pursuing a degree in fashion, and when he reached his last semester, they canceled his degree track and said he had to take two more semesters to graduate.

In short, he left with his education and no degree. How many of us went to schools that closed down? How many students have lost credits, money, and time because the school wasn't honest about the accreditation while they were attending?

My brother was devastated, like many of us, when the rug was snatched from beneath our feet.

INJUSTICE

He had to think about what he wanted to do and how much more he wanted to spend. To go forward was to spend thousands more, to stop was to lose tens of thousands. Either way, he felt stuck but decided to stop his degree and enjoy the education he paid for.

How many of us are dealing with the injustice caused by student loans for schools that didn't work for the money? Some of our education papers are not worth the cost of the ink used to print our names on them. The only thing it was good for was the memories and lessons we pulled away from it. The school, in the end, didn't help you find a job, provide adequate resources, or give you a leg up into anything but debt.

Now, my sister, over the years, has gotten several degrees, and I am sure more are in her future because of her passion for entering both fields. Now, she has finished her nail program and is licensed. She was working too many jobs and thought to go to one. She got hired at a salon that quickly sold it after hiring her.

She would drive to Timbuktu to make a few dollars or no money and come home. These positions treat you like a freelancer, but they dictate your time as if they paid you hourly. I think this is a huge injustice to make staff stay when you have no customers and your pay is solely based on customer compensation and not your time in the slightest.

To work and stay at a job with no pay, is criminal but also spiritually wrong. Jeremiah 22:13 says, "Woe to him who builds his house by unrighteousness, and his upper rooms by injustice, who makes his neighbor serve him for nothing and does not give him his wages." Ironically, both locations that had my sister working for free closed in a matter of months.

RELEASE PAIN

I am sure she wasn't the happiest camper to find out she had no job both times, and she was equally upset when the second company withheld her last three weeks of pay because she claimed my sister should understand her financial crisis. This woman had no tack when running her business, and I believe she burned a lot of wicks on all sides.

She hired our mother and grandfather and never paid them for the job they completed twice! They didn't have a contract to enforce in court, and if they went to court, they would have been suing a business that didn't exist anymore. She was over the salon and the pressure and responsibility. She left all her items in the shop and only told my sister the day she was leaving to grab what she wanted free of charge.

We both knew she was up to something, and she was. She planned to make that money swap for her pay, but she never vocalized that. She kept saying she would pay her week after week. Even crazier, one week she said for her to give items back so she could raise money and pay her from that! Who thinks anyone is dumb enough to move your stuff for free and then give it to you when they never got paid, they housed your stuff, and had to find a job with no notice because you didn't prepare them for your closing?

She was heartless, in my opinion, because she knew she had no other job and children to provide for. An injustice like this could be enough to set someone's whole life behind. It could be enough to make a person want to quit and think to go in a different direction altogether. It is enough to make a person turn their back on God, cus the person out in their heart, or even pray terrible things. It's enough to make you cry.

But my sister didn't quit. She took the items

INJUSTICE

and stored them in my mom's garage for a few days before a major door would open by Yah. He had our aunt help her to find a place and pay for the first week, and she started her business out of chaos. What was a grave injustice turned out to be the biggest push for her to stretch into her own business, Shea Nailed It!

Does that mean this was God's plan to push my sister into her business? That He wills bad things in our lives on purpose, that He permits injustice because of a malicious plan to use everything for our good? We can ask sometimes, "God, why would you allow me to lose my job? Why would you allow this or that to happen to me?"

Romans 9:14-18 records this, which brings me strength when bad things happen to welcome the good in my life.

"What shall we say then? Is there injustice on God's part? By no means! 15 For he says to Moses, "I will have mercy on whom I have mercy, and I will have compassion on whom I have compassion." 16 So then it depends not on human will or exertion, but on God, who has mercy. 17 For the Scripture says to Pharaoh, "For this very purpose I have raised you up, that I might show my power in you, and that my name might be proclaimed in all the earth. 18 So then He has mercy on whomever He wills, and He hardens whomever He wills."

RELEASE PAIN

We know that God is the creator of justice, so that makes Him the standard of what is good and just. It can be hard to accept some of the decisions Yah makes, and we can think that His choice is unfair or even unjust. However, He is the only holy One who has never failed nor committed a sin. He never had a breach against His own Word but is perfect. We can read in the Word that His ways are higher than ours (Isaiah 55:8-9).

Although we can be hurting from choices and circumstances that are unfair or unjust, take courage with these verses of power and justice. The good news is that there is no one above the judgment seat of Yah. Those who have money are equal to those who do not. The mercy seat of Yah can see men and women from every walk at His feet. Coming to Him is not reserved for the poor but for everyone who needs to release injustice or plead for forgiveness for their injustice.

If we commit an injustice against ourselves, it could be quickly defined as ignoring the Voice and Word of Yah to do what we want to do. If He says to leave, we must trust Him because if we stay, we may have to live out the consequences not meant for us. When Adam and Eve believed the serpent, they took part in his judgment and also fell from their original design. However, they did not completely remove the grace of Yah from their lives.

We have hope of redemption! No matter where you are, you can receive the helping hand of Yah to bring healing where injustice was growing to become a cancer set on destroying your hope for a God-approved future. So, no matter what it looks like, you will win!

EMPOWERING SCRIPTURES: INJUSTICE

Micah 2:1-2 Woe to those who devise wickedness and work evil on their beds! When the morning dawns, they perform it because it is in the power of their hand. 2 They covet fields and seize them, and houses, and take them away; they oppress a man and his house, a man and his inheritance.

1 Timothy 1:9 understanding this, that the law is not laid down for the just but for the lawless and disobedient, for the ungodly and sinners, for the unholy and profane, for those who strike their fathers and mothers, for murderers,

1 Peter 1:16 since it is written, "You shall be holy, for I am holy."

Jeremiah 22:13 Woe to him who builds his house by unrighteousness, and his upper rooms by injustice, who makes his neighbor serve him for nothing and does not give him his wages,

Job 5:16 So the poor have hope, and injustice shuts her mouth.

Job 11:14 If iniquity is in your hand, put it far away, and let not injustice dwell in your tents.

Proverbs 13:23 The fallow ground of the poor would yield much food, but it is swept away through injustice.

Proverbs 16:8 Better is a little with righteousness than great revenues with injustice.

Romans 9:13-18 As it is written, "Jacob I loved, but Esau I hated." 14 What shall we say then? Is there injustice on God's part? By no means! 15 For he says to Moses, "I will have mercy on whom I have mercy, and I will have compassion on whom I have compassion." 16 So then it depends not on human will or exertion, but on God, who has mercy. 17 For the Scripture says to Pharaoh, "For this very purpose I have raised you up, that I might show my power in you, and that my name might be proclaimed in all the earth." 18 So then he has mercy on whomever he wills, and he hardens whomever he wills.

Luke 12:57-59 And why do you not judge for yourselves what is right? 58 As you go with your accuser before the magistrate, make an effort to settle with him on the way, lest he drags you to the judge, and the judge hands you over to the officer, and the officer puts you in prison. 59 I tell you, you will never get out until you have paid the very last penny.

Isaiah 55:11 ...so shall my word be that goes out from my mouth; it shall not return to me empty, but it shall accomplish that which I purpose and shall succeed in the thing for which I sent it.

Proverbs 22:8 Whoever sows injustice will reap calamity, and the rod of his fury will fail.

Proverbs 17:15 He who justifies the wicked and he who condemns the righteous are both alike an abomination to the Lord.

2 Chronicles 19:7 Now then, let the fear of the Lord be upon you. Be careful what you do, for there is no injustice with the Lord our God, or partiality or taking bribes."

INJUSTICE

Leviticus 19:15 You shall do no injustice in court. You shall not be partial to the poor or defer to the great, but in righteousness shall you judge your neighbor.

Ecclesiastes 5:8 If you see in a province the oppression of the poor and the violation of justice and righteousness, do not be amazed at the matter, for the high official is watched by a higher, and there are yet higher ones over them.

Matthew 27:24 So when Pilate saw that he was gaining nothing, but rather that a riot was beginning, he took water and washed his hands before the crowd, saying, "I am innocent of this man's blood; see to it yourselves."

YOUR POWER AND
FOUNDATION

One thing about the Word of God is that it will never turn to Him void (not happen) but will accomplish what He sends it out to do (Isiah 55:11). He says that whoever sows injustice will reap calamity, and the rod of his fury will fail (Proverbs 22:8). I know we have all been watching the unraveling of many public figures who grow to prominence in music.

They had status, money, power, and influence. They had friends in high places who knew how to hide their crimes and ungodly acts. Like how Ecclesiastes 5:8 says, " If you see in a province the oppression of the poor and the violation of justice and righteousness, do not be amazed at the matter, for the high official is watched by a higher, and there are yet higher ones over them."

However, as I have said before in my book The Ecstasy, the devil has no friends. He uses people for as long as he can, and then he throws them away, usually penniless and begging for a lifeline. The devil and evil spirits don't like humanity, but they use us like many think to use them by playing with witchcraft and occult behaviors.

These artists and millionaires are being busted for raping children, beating women, and molesting boys and men. They are being uncovered for eating children and performing other occult acts in private and public. Selling your soul might have been popular, but the judgment of these actives is also growing. Sheep that have led the church away have also been ousted in public and suffering publicly for their crimes against Yah and man.

He would not be just if He did not judge. Choosing to have mercy on who He chooses is His choice. He can love Jacob and "hate" Esau (Malachi 1:3 and Romans 9:13). I know there are people married to men or women violating people and causing all kinds of injustice. For some spouses, they separate themselves. Businessmen and women decide they no longer want to partner with unethical people.

It is wise to separate yourselves from people who are hellbent on their own vengeance. It is wise

INJUSTICE

to wash your hands of injustice like Pilate (Matthew 27:24). Anyone who justifies the wicked and he who condemns the righteous are both alike an abomination to the Lord (Proverbs 17:15). We have all heard of the trials where the criminal got away.

In the eyes of Yah, crooked people in any seat can be judged. He is the great judge who judges all people, no matter their title. He will avenge all injustice, and as we say in common speech, "Every dog has their day." We don't have to pray for judgment, but we can thank the Father for His justice. He knows the right answer: punishment or grace.

For the lawyers who defended known and habitual criminals, some of which were thrown into jail on charges for how they bullied people into gag orders. Juries that were bought or pushed to rule because of a person's skin and presumed poverty, or picking a person to fit the bill of a crime they didn't commit, don't go unnoticed by Yah.

Judges and cops are not immune to making mistakes, but they should be warned. Leviticus 19:15 says, "You shall do no injustice in court. You shall not be partial to the poor or defer to the great, but in righteousness shall you judge your neighbor." Chronicles 19:7 further says, "Now then, let the fear of the Lord be upon you. Be careful what you do, for there is no injustice with the Lord our God or partiality for taking bribes."

Committing injustice may feel good for a season, but no matter what you do, no matter what deals you strike, there is a cost. When you do one thing to hide something, it starts the rabbit-hole effect. The best place to be is on the just side, even though it may come with trials. Your soul is in tack, and your mind, will, and emotions are free to live again when we release the pain we feel.

RELEASE PAIN

I know some of us who have lost big and might have thought of killing someone even as a thought with no intention of bringing it to fruition. Stay clear of thoughts like these. The enemy will use this pain and frustration to create a monster that you will not be able to easily maintain. The spirit of rage can be sparked, and it is hard to quench. I wrote a novel about a woman who hid her pain, and her inner thoughts and decisions created a "monster." Read about her unraveling and the trail of tears she left behind on her road to redemption and accountability. There is an answer to our behavior and choices, and not all of them will be what we like.

But there is a God that can release the pain you feel from injustice and right all wrongs. Trust His guiding Hand and infinite grace, mercy, and goodness.

INJUSTICE

Release Pain

Unfaithful

UNFAITHFUL

Raise your hand if you can stand a liar. How many people want to be friends with a liar? What about marrying, dating, or hanging out with them? I am sure all of us have our hands down because no one wants to hang out with someone who is a liar.

Liars can be people who brag about things they do not have, which is one of the most annoying versions of it. These people go out of their way to create stories that will have the listener fall in love with a fantasy. How many of us know this daydream is more like a nightmare? All the plans you thought you had can come tumbling down when the foundation of those plans was based on the words of a liar.

We don't always know we are being sold a pipedream, do we? Sometimes the information sounds really good, so good, it is hard to believe it is true. When we want or need something so desperately to be true, we can believe a lie without hesitation. We can dream with the speaker and hope that what they are saying is true.

Have you ever signed up for a business and thought you were going to make money by doing something simple or nothing at all? I remember we signed up for this paper envelope gig back in the day. It sounded real good. You can work from home by sealing up envelopes and mailing them off. It was simple, and a person with children could have a sweat-house going in minutes.

We had ambitions to work our own hours and select how much we would do for pay. So, nothing unethical. However, as we started working and got things cranked out, there was a snag. The company shipped the materials to us. We had to pay a fee, of course, to sign up. When we thought the request for mailers would come in, they never did!

We all were excited about working to make some money, but the money never came. What about the time your parent(s) said they would take you somewhere? You know, it could be somewhere like the movies, a game, or maybe even them coming to a game or event you were having.

Did you keep checking the door? Were you on pins and needles as you sat on the porch watching traffic and people go by? You were putting your best emotions forward to see this promise fulfilled, but for whatever reason, the event and time together were canceled. You left the space you were standing, sad, to say the least.

For some of us, we left angry. We started to come up with a plan for what we would do to show our frustration. We started getting lippy with people at the event. We were aggressive to the people who were present. We missed the chance to enjoy our event because our focus was on the liar. The one who said they would come and did not.

Have you ever been there? Have you ever come up with a plan for your own justice when someone lies to you? The Bible tells us, "Do not lie," but for some of us, it is not something we can easily stop doing (Leviticus 19:11 and Exodus 20:16).

UNFAITHFUL

What makes it so difficult for people to guard their tongue and not say what may be easy for them to say, a lie?

Fear of disappointment, I have found, causes many to lie. When we are put on the spot it can be tempting to tell a lie to avoid the fallout of telling the truth. I know we have all been in a tight spot with a parent, and when they asked, "Did you do this?" We all want to say "no," no matter the truth, because we don't want to disappoint them. We don't want to make them angrier either.

I tell my children, "Don't lie to me. I do not like lying, and Yah doesn't either. If you will lie, you will steal. If you will do that, you don't care about nobody but yourself." Those who lie don't see a problem with how their lies will catch up to them until they are caught and have to pay the price. They enjoy the instant reward of avoiding trouble no matter how long the wave lasts for.

Lying doesn't get you away from trouble; it only delays your judgment. People who think they have a benefit from lying tend to lie more often. Or, to hide one lie, they have to keep on lying. What does that sound like to you? It sounds like you got the first hit seemingly for free, and now the addictive behavior will cost you more each time!

Some people have become addicted to lying, and we are innocent people in their web of deception. What I don't sign up for is co-signing someone else's lies. If you lie, that is on you, but please don't bring me into it. I think it is sad when parents may unintentionally teach their children to lie to them by asking them to lie for them.

Deuteronomy 7:4 says, "For they will turn away thy son from following me, that they may serve other gods: so will the anger of the LORD be

kindled against you, and destroy thee suddenly."
While you think you are using your children to help you out, the enemy is using you to teach your children to lie. As parents, what our children see us do speaks louder than what they hear us say. It is in the small details that we learn lying is harmless and believe if it doesn't hurt anyone, it is fine.

People can lie to spare people's feelings. But is it really that they are sparing someone else's feelings, or do they not want to put in the time to communicate and help resolve what might be an issue? If someone is having a bad day, you don't have to be rude about the hair, but honesty does help. You can help them find a solution and be part of a solution rather than lying to get out of doing anything.

Laziness can trigger lying, most assuredly. However, most of us lie to get out of responsibility. We don't want to own up to the pain or criticism we deserve or may need to correct a behavior. Children are guilty of lying more so because they don't want to receive a punishment for what they did wrong.

But as I have said in the book Mothering Spirit, we are all children in the sight of Yah. We are all guilty of wanting to get out of trouble, and it can be easy for us to lie to ourselves if we don't want to be held accountable. The easiest lie we tell morphs as an excuse. We say we don't want to do this because it is raining. But the truth is if we wanted something bad enough, we would stand in the snow to get it.

We say we fell out of love, and this is why we don't want a relationship anymore. The truth, we never loved them in that way, and what we married them for, they no longer have or we can't settle any longer. It could be looks, money, job, influence, importance, or something else. We can say we want a college degree and quit the program because we blame it on our children and other responsibilities. The truth is that we can achieve a degree and work if we learn to balance our lives, but that might not be something we want to do.

In essence, we become unfaithful when we are not committed wholeheartedly to something or someone. When we are not committed to a relationship of any kind, we will find a reason to excuse ourselves from being present. We can try to lie to ourselves for why we don't show up, but the truth is that we are not committed enough if we pull out excuses to justify our behavior.

I know the people who lie habitually think they are getting brownie points by saying the right thing when they already know they have no intentions of doing a thing. Proverbs 12:22 says, "Lying lips are an abomination to the Lord, but those who act faithfully are his delight." Flattery will get you nowhere with Yah. Similarly, to how lying to a person who knows you can smell your lies from a far off, and they may only smile and nod to politely dismiss you, He can silence your words and even prayers.

Don't we all delight in the truth, especially when a person says they will do something and they do it? Who wants to be in a relationship with a person or have a parent who lies all of the time? I know of a person who had a parent who would lie and say all kinds of stuff they never would do. They would promise trips, gifts, visits, and events that simply never happened.

At the time of their commitment, the child was elated to hear the news. They waited for them. When things didn't pan out, they didn't get discouraged because the parent had an excuse for why they couldn't make it. They claimed traffic, hospital visits, deaths in the family, and anything else they could use. When they claimed a death in the family, they didn't even go to the funeral that was on that day. They simply want to do what they want and will lean on any excuse to do just that.

People who lie may feel like they are getting away from accountability. Their lying makes them think the extension of the rope people give them to make good on their word will always be there. How many of them don't know that "Truthful lips endure forever, but a lying tongue is but for a moment" (Proverbs 12:19)? That child who used to get so excited to hear from their father stopped taking their calls.

He didn't want to give the parent the time of day to say one word to him that would give him hope in his character or actions. The getting of treasures by a lying tongue is a fleeting vapor and a snare of death (Proverbs 21:6). What you think you are stealing from someone through lying will not last. When you tell lies to tell people you will do something and don't, it does not build your name, but it shuts you out.

When parents often lie to their children, the relationship between them is breaking down. The Bible says it is better not to vow a thing than to vow and not pay (Ecclesiastes 5:5). When we say we are going to do something; it is important that we follow through and only seldom miss the mark. If you find that you cannot keep a promise or your word, stop freely extending it. Instead, only vow what you will do or don't vow a thing at all and be full of healthy surprises.

The pain that can be inflicted on hearts when parents have habitually let us down can hurt us to our core. We can want to believe for greater, but we could have been conditioned to see men or women as liars because of our relationship with

UNFAITHFUL

one or both of our parents. Our parents are the first relationship we have with the world, and if that relationship is tainted, it can warp our ideas about genders.

Do you feel you have held some of the resentment, disappointment, or pain against a parent toward others? Sometimes, we can hold our future relationships hostage because we are afraid we will get let down, like when we were a child. We can be angry toward men or women because of something they didn't do to us, but because of the unfaithfulness of someone else. We can hold other people accountable for the lies we were told in past relationships and our treatment of others is completely unfair.

We don't want to hold our parents in emotional jail in our hearts. We don't want to limit our future because we were disappointed by our parents. We don't want to see our future through the lens of our past. Our relationships do impact us, however, and they inadvertently impact how we see the world. What we want to do so that we don't give the devil or evil spirits glory is to disallow the enemy to take our relationships and rob us of creating healthy boundaries.

With people who we cannot so easily get away from, like parents and ex's we share children with, we need to establish a healthy bond. We need to be able to forgive them for their offenses, lies, and unfaithfulness to us and not allow that experience to negatively impact what we desire from a healthy partnership with other members of our family. This includes relationships with grandparents, and not allowing your relationship with your parents to impede on your children's ability to see a different side of them.

I knew of a woman who said, "All men lie."

I am sure you have heard women and men say this, too. Some say it, and they honestly believe it, and they use it to justify how they treat the men they are dating. I have also heard things like, we are not married, so I am free to do what I want. Many men don't get married because they want to lean on this saying to justify their sleeping around, "I ain't married to her. She ain't my wife."

I have read this verse several times in the Bible, but I have never taken the time to look up what it means–until now. I wasn't sure of what Balaam worship was or what it implies. I did some research because the name pops up a lot in the Bible to see what God's offense would be with this kind of worship.

In Revelation 2:14, He says, "Nevertheless, I have a few things against you: There are some among you who hold to the teaching of Balaam, who taught Balak to entice the Israelites." The ideas of Balaam, a devil worshiper or sorcerer, depending on which book you read, encourage Balaak to teach the Israelites to compromise their beliefs under the guise that a little sin won't do great harm. A little sin can be beneficial if it leads to prosperity, personal gain of some kind, or sexual gratification.

Balaam's agenda was to encourage women to seduce men to likely attend orgies, venues, or feasts where there would be alcohol or drugs and other vile or perverse things happening. Business dealings that happen would be attached to some level of immorality. A modern interpretation of this would be going to strip clubs to talk business!

The evil union of performing or engaging in activities unholy would serve as the yoke to keep violators of God in check. As long as you obey, attend, take bribes, enjoy the women, or whatever, you could party with the big boys. Balaam and

UNFAITHFUL

those practicing his doctrine will encourage women and men to defile themselves by performing acts that are against holy principles.

What I have come to realize is that it is not innocent when we engage in parties, actions, drinking, smoking, doing drugs, or habits that open doors to the occult. We might not realize that the choices we are making are bringing us subject to the manipulation and control of an evil spirit. Sometimes, we simply think it is fun, and I am out to have a good time and explore what life has to offer. People think it is fun to have multiple women and to explore sexually deviant behavior because the world tells us a little fun won't hurt us.

Too often, we get caught up in the drug of sexual sin, the high of getting something for nothing or compromising our beliefs for the early payoff of getting what we want for the moment. Feeding this microwave desire to be happy can lead to a lifetime of pain. Many who prove to be unfaithful in their marriages were tripped up or seduced by sexual perversion or other deviant behavior.

Fifty percent of marriages that are ending in divorce are divorcing because of social media, computers, phones, and connecting with people on the internet. People are giving up their real relationships for fantasies, uncertain of reality; they are making life choices unaware of if they are even being catfished online. What would make a person cheat through text messaging?

What lie would you need to believe or images you likely entertained that would allow you to be comfortable to part ways with your spouse and children? People are willing to throw away their lives, marriages, and futures for men or women they don't know anything about. If we think for a second that their are only good people in the world, we would be grossly incorrect.

Witches are real. Angels are real. The devil is real. Evil spirits are real. Yah, God Almighty is real. If all this is true, what would that imply? There are people fighting for both sides to impact how we live our lives. There is God who says, "There are six things that the Lord hates, seven that are an abomination to Him: haughty eyes, a lying tongue, and hands that shed innocent blood, a heart that devises wicked plans, feet that make haste to run to evil, a false witness who breathes out lies, and one who sows discord among brothers" (Proverbs 6:16-19).

The Father doesn't like lying. He doesn't like those who lie to obtain something ill-gotten from someone else. He doesn't like stealing. He doesn't like people who are messy, devising plans, scheming to have brothers turn against each other. The ones who are quick to come up with plans to have the innocent hurt, harmed, or afflicted–bother Him.

When people think they are doing God a favor by lying to their wives, children, family, coworkers, and employees to honor Him, they are wrong. The Father is not pleased when we use lying as a weapon to rob or steal the choices people could make for their lives. If you have been a victim of someone lying to you, like I have, it is not a good feeling.

I know it can be tempting to do to them what they did to you. If they cheated on you, an evil spirit would be right there to encourage you to make them pay for the pain you feel. That voice could tell you to do to them the same thing they did you. It can pump us up to feel validated for violating Yah's decrees because of someone being unfaithful to us. This spirit would make us believe that someone else's unfaithfulness is good reason for our

UNFAITHFUL

unfaithfulness to God or ourselves.

As believers, we are to live Colossians 3:9-10 which says, "Do not lie to one another, seeing that you have put off the old self with its practices, and have put on the new self, which is being renewed in knowledge after the image of its Creator." It can be hard to overlook unfaithfulness. Even when we say we forgive, it can be hard to forget. It can be hard to accept the reason or the lack thereof for why a person treated us like they did. It can be hard to go back to the way things were and, honestly, they will never be the same.

The breach is something that won't be forgotten and the truth, what if you don't have to forget about what happened to move on? What if you don't and shouldn't bury what happened, but you must decide to speak about it and allow the healing to take place? Whatever was broken between the two of you or missing, now is the time to fill that gap with something greater. Fallouts can be a reason you can fall into new patterns that are healthier and maybe the way your relationship should have been all along.

How exactly can you be set free from pain after unfaithfulness? I know of a couple who had been together for nearly three decades. They were not close and their commitment to each other was one-sided. She said they loved each other, but what may have lied beneath could bring questions. He was not a particularly nice man to her.

If I am honest, the man was more like a pimp to her when they first met. He was aggressive, abusive, demanding, and controlling. She married him because she said she always loved him. She was willing to sell herself to make him happy. She never had children. She was pregnant once but lost the baby and was fearful to have any more.

She decided in her own heart that she was not fit or ready to ever be a mother, especially with her husband. Eventually, she got out of that line of work. She went to church and a lot of her life patterns were changed. The witchcraft she learned from her mother, yes, her mom was a practicing witch, she disowned to follow Yah. There is nothing too hard for Yah.

She was set free from the life of running the streets, doing drugs, and selling her body. She wanted to give up the lifestyle that her husband liked. He liked that she liked girls and was okay with orgies whenever he wanted them. There was a problem in their marriage all along because he never respected her and saw her true value. He liked that he could control her and make her do anything from this devotion she had to him.

Her devotion did not make him nicer, faithful, or loving. His personality did not change when her life changed. He didn't mind her going to church and getting involved but he never made an attempt to come closer to God. He remained on the outside of the will of God for the life they could have lived together. She remained by his side, praying for him, but he would get angry, cuss her out, beat her up, and tell her to stop praying for him. She didn't leave him no matter what he did, so he had no boundaries but did whatever he desired. He knew in his heart she would do nothing about it.

The love for him was not as passionate after the years had gone by but grew dull. Her devotion to him turned to fear of him. She couldn't leave him because she was afraid of what he would do, not because she saw a future with him. The love in this marriage grew very dry, if not non-existent in their last decade together. She was comfortable working in a domestic capacity, and he was okay with her keeping "his" house clean. They had an arrange-

UNFAITHFUL

ment that worked. He had many women who she would find in his phone, and ultimately found out he had a child with another woman.

After finding this out, she did not leave him but remained faithful to him still. He wasn't happy about her decision to give her life to God, but he did tolerate it. He didn't ask her to participate in the threesomes anymore, but he did have them without her. When the baby was discovered, he blamed her for not being there and said maybe this was the baby she could never give him. He made it as if he was doing her a favor!

When you are low, and someone who is supposed to love you kicks you down low, it hurts. It hurt her heart to be with a man who was so cruel to her, but there was an oath in her heart that she could not break. She grew to believe Yah wanted her to live like this. That God got honor and glory out of a relationship that was absent of Love, patience, kindness, goodness, and forgiveness. Do you think that God would be pleased with a connection, an unholy union like this?

She felt obligated to him before the church and after encountering Yah. She could not undo the marriage and battled many times about leaving him. She stayed with him until he died of a long-term illness. After his death, she didn't celebrate her freedom. She longed for the pain she was familiar with. The uncultured love bred out of pain was her go-to to explain what love was, although she knew it was contrary to the Word of God.

It is hard to believe that God is a good God when you choose to see His word contrary to His intention. Yes, marriages are work. Yes, there will be highs and lows and even periods you may have to separate. We cannot, however, expect Yah to hold a marriage together that He never joined.

RELEASE PAIN

Can He do it? Yes, nothing is too hard–but will He? That is a choice He chooses to make. The good part, as a child of His, He will tell you His plans and desires for your life, but will you take action on His Word to release the pain you are carrying?

She had plans to leave him, perhaps knowing that Yah wanted more for her. He released her from the relationship that caused her so much pain, but she wanted pain more than real Love. Yet, even after his death, I cannot say she has released the pain she has felt over three decades. Thirty years of suffering is a long time. Like many of us, we may choose to stay with a spouse who cheated or cheats on us. My second husband had this problem, but I refused to subject myself to the risk and the pain.

I can relate to wanting something to work so badly and not be a failure. The first marriage was hard, and the second was harder. It was not because my separation was hard; we lived more apart than we did together during our marriage. What was hard was for me to accept I picked wrong or that I did not have what I was believing Yah for, again.

We don't always know what to do with our hurt, so we try to suppress it. To ignore it and pretend it never happened, thinking this will downplay the pain you feel. That it would hide the guilt, torment, and disappointment you feel within yourself for the marriage ending.

If you were the cause, you too can carry pain that the Father can heal you from. It is not just the ones who were the victims who need Yah. It is the ones who also caused the pain who need to heal. When we let people down, it can impact how we see ourselves and determine if we can trust ourselves.

UNFAITHFUL

We can see many who are at fault for changing their marriage getting angry about the state of their marriage. They expect the spouse to get over it, and some even demand that they do so the two of them can move on. They come up with excuses like, "She was just a booty call. She didn't mean anything. Or it was a mistake while I was drunk."

The Bible says, "The good person out of the good treasure of his heart produces good, and the evil person out of his evil treasure produces evil, for out of the abundance of the heart his mouth speaks" (Luke 6:45). When you listen to people you can understand where they are by what they speak about. When people want to move past sensitive topics or change the subject of your pain to deflect their pain, they are hiding.

Going around a subject is like hiding in the dark. They want to pile on confusion and blame, add in points that are not directly relevant, and silence the behaviors and thoughts that contributed to the breach. The truth, no one just wakes up one day and determines to cheat on their spouse. No one. Also, no one allows their senses to dull enough to be taken advantage of or to choose to cross the line without a conscious decision at some point in the process unless they were raped.

It is like saying you can drive a car without putting the key in the ignition, turning it on, or letting the car run. You cannot. The car requires a series of events to occur to trigger the machine to work. Marriage requires a series of events to happen to allow a union to take place. Unfaithfulness also requires a series of events to take place before it can manifest.

So what was broken? What small foxes have crept in and corrupted the good vine (Song of Solomon 2:15)? Was it evil communication that ruined good manners (1 Corinthians 15:33-34)? Was it a lie that the enemy said or an experience that gave them or you confidence or validation to get what you wanted?

A little leaven, leavens the whole loaf (1 Corinthians 5:6). A little lie, we don't notice at the time, starts to break down the entire marriage. Staying out here and there, acting single in your heart, and believing that there is better out there for you all leads to a mindset and lifestyle that opens the door to unfaithfulness.

The real reason someone is unfaithful is the lust of the eyes, lust of the flesh (sexual), and the pride of life (John 2:16). There is a strong disdain that can build in us because we have allowed the whispers of evil spirits to bewitch us. We don't know that the enticement of sexual immorality is linked to witchcraft. We don't see the evil spirit, so we think it is us, our mind, our thoughts. We take on their essence and believe in their words more than the Word.

We exchange the Gospel, the message of the Bible, for the lust of the flesh, the lust of the eyes, and the pride of life. We have been bewitched, as Paul insinuates in Galatians Chapter 3 when he writes:

"O foolish Galatians! Who has bewitched you? It was before your eyes that Jesus Christ was publicly portrayed as crucified. 2 Let me ask you only this: Did you receive the Spirit by works of the law or by hearing with faith? 3 Are you so foolish? Having begun by the Spirit, are you now being perfected by the flesh?

4 Did you suffer so many things in vain—if indeed it was in vain? 5 Does he who supplies the Spirit to you and works miracles among you do so

UNFAITHFUL

by works of the law, or by hearing with faith— 6 just as Abraham "believed God, and it was counted to him as righteousness?"

7 Know then that it is those of faith who are the sons of Abraham. 8 And the Scripture, foreseeing that God would justify the Gentiles by faith, preached the gospel beforehand to Abraham, saying, "In you shall all the nations be blessed." 9 So then, those who are of faith are blessed along with Abraham, the man of faith."

Have we not all witnessed a miracle from God? It is not the children of darkness that we contend with the most, but those who say they believe. Those who claim they believe in God who are the ones running after the lust of the world. Those who go to church but live contrary. Those who demand people pray before their food, but they don't follow the sacrificial lifestyle set before them in the Word. Those who believe in putting their hand on the Bible when in court but won't speak the Word when they are confronted with unholy acts of bribery, sexual immorality, or other lust.

We have been witnesses of Yah's goodness, but what pulls us away from His goodness? What blinds us–even bewitching us to no longer see the power in living holy? We say petty things like, "Living right is boring." I love how Pastor Stephen defined boring. He says boring is you not wanting to do what you should do, so you claim to be bored, which is a rebellious heart toward doing what you were told to do. Instead of being faithful to work you decide to sit and do nothing out of your rebellious spirit.

Instead of taking the woman to dinner who you picked and finding new ways to love her, you claim she is boring. Is she boring, or has your lust for other women increased? Has the lust of the man destined to be unfaithful been seduced by spirits that cling together like sexual perversion, alcohol, drugs, addiction, and rage taken him over?

We were able to lean on faith and not our actions from what we deserved to see miracles. When we need something we cannot buy or earn, and Yah gives it to us, it lifts our hearts and changes our lives. For the moment, our houses are swept clean, we are released from the snares of the enemy, and it feels beautiful (Matthew 12:43-45). The issue that will soon come is when the Father comes in and saves the day; if we don't continue with what He starts, we lose it. The spiritual attack we got rest from is now back with a vengeance as it is written.

Matthew 12:43-45 says, "When the unclean spirit has gone out of a person, it passes through waterless places seeking rest, but finds none. 44 Then it says, 'I will return to my house from which I came.' And when it comes, it finds the house empty, swept, and put in order. 45 Then it goes and brings with it seven other spirits more evil than itself, and they enter and dwell there, and the last state of that person is worse than the first. So also will it be with this evil generation."

If you doubt that unfaithfulness is a manifestation of witchcraft, I want to show you the evidence. In Luke 8:17 it reads, "For nothing is hidden that will not be made manifest, nor is anything secret that will not be known and come to light." In 1 John 8:44, it says, "You are of your father the devil, and your will is to do your father's desires. He was a murderer from the beginning and does not stand in the truth because there is no truth in him. When he lies, he speaks out of his own character, for he is a liar and the father of lies."

The first step you have to believe is a lie. You have to believe you don't have it all. You have

UNFAITHFUL

to believe someone is not good enough, you don't have enough, you deserve more, etc. It begins with you listening to the father of lies. You then buy into this doctrine and start lying to cover your covenant with the father of lies.

So if you are lying to your wife, lying to your friends, lying to the woman believing that this is righteous, good, or will make you happy, you have exchanged the Truth for a lie. The Word says in John 14:6, "Yashua said to him, "I am the way, and the truth, and the life. No one comes to the Father except through Me." We cannot get to Yah or be a child of His without believing and making a covenant with the Word of God, who is Jesus, Yashua! Yashua is the Word of God (John 1:1).

You can only have one Father. You cannot have two Fathers according to Yah, the Creator of heaven and earth. When He created humanity, as believers, we receive that He made Adam and Eve male and female. He did not make Adam and three more women. Adam looked at Eve and said it was good. He didn't complain he needed more, she did! Then, they both agreed and succumbed to a lie.

The DNA of their children could only point to one father. The Son of God could only have one Father He was not linked through two or three. The fathering spirit is real, and that is the Spirit of fatherhood that Yah put in the earth to guide man. Read more about this in the book and the Mothering Spirit if you want to unpack this more.

But let us press on; you can only have one father. You either take on the Word of Yah as your foundation, or you call Him a liar and believe your way is greater, and worse, the ways of fallen angels and the devil himself is greater. They tempt you with the lust of the eyes, flesh, and the pride of life. They tried to tempt Yashua all the same. You think they didn't throw up pretty women, naked women, money, prestige, and a natural kingdom?

He turned it all down because it did not come from Yah but was a covenant He would be making with the devil in exchange for the powerful one He had with God the Father. He knew this father of lies was calling the Truth of Yah lesser than what he could provide to appease the flesh, the eyes, and a man's ego. He saw the game, and He played the only hand He had; he used the Word to confound the liar.

Can you, or those you love, learn to deny themselves? Do you have a desire, or should we pray that the Father puts the desire within your heart? If you are battling with unfaithfulness, you are going to have to go into spiritual warfare. You will have to bind spirits, cancel covenants, and choose the Word of Yah over the lies of the enemy.

You cannot hold on to the enemy's things and think God wants to use them for His glory. He wants you to cast down every imagination that rises against the knowledge of Yah (2 Corinthians 2:5). Everything that would say no to His plans for your life, marriage, business, family, or personal growth. Any spirit whispering actions, thoughts, or ideas contrary to the Knowledge, hence, the Word of Yah, we are to cast down, bind, and send back to hell. He wants all of you to be filled with His Word and Spirit!

UNFAITHFUL

The enemy will tell you that you can withhold a little from God, and He won't miss it. This is Balaam worship. You can give Yah what you want and hold on to what you choose. This is not what the Word of God says. We are called bondservants of Christ (1 Corinthians 7:22). To be a bondservant is to be a slave to Christ. To be a slave to Christ is to be a slave to the Word. Yashua, the Christ is the Word! However! To be a bondservant of Christ is to be free because the Word sets the captives free (John 8:36, Luke 4:18)!

They will convince you that a little sin won't hurt anything. But sin is never satisfied (Proverbs 27:20). Have you noticed one lie leads to a million? It leads to confusion. Some people tell so many lies that they don't know the truth anymore. They can't keep their lies straight.

Wherever there is confusion, there are lies. Yah is not the author of confusion (1 Corinthians 14:33) or the father of lies. The devil will never tell you the truth. So if he has told you, a little sin won't hurt. Doing this one time won't really change your life. If you know his character, you already know he is lying to you. If you wonder if God is telling you to sin, and so if you sin, you are doing Him a favor, be comforted by this. James 1:13 says, "Let no one say when he is tempted, "I am being tempted by God," for God cannot be tempted with evil, and He Himself tempts no one."

For those unfaithful, they need to realize they are not speaking to themselves. They are not speaking to Yah! They are not having innocent fun. They are playing with the things of the devil, the father of lies. They are making bargains with the enemy's devices and to partner with him is not freedom. But oh, they can bring the things you want at a cost.

Nothing is free, and the penalty of bartering with the devil and evil spirits is death! Sin once it is full grown brings death. James 1:14-16 says, "But each person is tempted when he is lured and enticed by his own desire. 15 Then desire, when it has conceived, gives birth to sin, and sin, when it is fully grown, brings forth death. 16 Do not be deceived, my beloved brothers [and sisters]."

The enemy comes to kill, steal, and destroy (John 10:10). If you are listening to the father of lies and being unfaithful, entertaining the doctrines of evil spirits and witches, he will destroy your house. His job is to kill, steal, and destroy. He wants your happiness, hope, fun, good times, good memories, and etc. When you are miserable, he is happy. So you have to take back your dominion!

You have to fight for your family, life, mind, spirit, marriage, and what you hold dear. Not by picking up weapons that are carnal, but the weapons of our warfare are not carnal but mighty, having divine power to pull down strongholds (2 Corinthians 10:4).

EMPOWERING SCRIPTURES: INJUSTICE

James 1:14-16 says, But each person is tempted when he is lured and enticed by his own desire. 15 Then desire, when it has conceived, gives birth to sin, and sin, when it is fully grown, brings forth death. 16 Do not be deceived, my beloved brothers [and sisters].

John 8:36 For he who was called in the Lord as a bondservant is a freedman of the Lord. Likewise he who was free when called is a bondservant of Christ.

Luke 4:18 The Spirit of the Lord is upon me, because he has anointed me to proclaim good news to the poor. He has sent me to proclaim liberty to the captives and recovering of sight to the blind, to set at liberty those who are oppressed

1 Corinthians 7:22 For he who was called in the Lord as a bondservant is a freedman of the Lord. Likewise, he who was free when called is a bondservant of Christ.

1 Corinthians 10:5 We destroy arguments and every lofty opinion raised against the knowledge of God, and take every thought captive to obey Christ

Song of Solomon 2:15 Catch the foxes for us, the little foxes that spoil the vineyards, for our vineyards are in blossom.

1 Corinthians 5:6 Your boasting is not good. Do you not know that a little leaven leavens the whole lump?

James 1:13 Let no one say when he is tempted, "I am being tempted by God," for God cannot be tempted with evil, and he himself tempts no one.

John 10:10 The thief comes only to steal and kill and destroy. I came that they may have life and have it abundantly.

John 14:6 Jesus said to him, "I am the way, and the truth, and the life. No one comes to the Father except through me.

John 1:1 In the beginning was the Word, and the Word was with God, and the Word was

God.

Deuteronomy 7:4 For they will turn away thy son from following me, that they may serve other gods: so will the anger of the LORD be kindled against you, and destroy thee suddenly.

Proverbs 12:22 Lying lips are an abomination to the Lord, but those who act faithfully are his delight.

Ecclesiastes 5:5 It is better that you should not vow than that you should vow and not pay. The good person out of the good treasure of his heart produces good, and the evil person out of his evil treasure produces evil, for out of the abundance of the heart his mouth speaks (Luke 6:45).

1 John 2:16 For all that is in the world—the desires of the flesh and the desires of the eyes and pride of life—is not from the Father but is from the world.

Matthew 12:43-45 When the unclean spirit has gone out of a person, it passes through waterless places seeking rest, but finds none. 44 Then it says, 'I will return to my house from which I came.' And when it comes, it finds the house empty, swept, and put in order. 45 Then it goes and brings with it seven other spirits more evil than itself, and they enter and dwell there, and the last state of that person is worse than the first. So also will it be with this evil generation."

Revelation 2:14 But I have a few things against you: you have some there who hold the teaching of Balaam, who taught Balak to put a stumbling block before the sons of Israel, so that they might eat food sacrificed to idols and practice sexual immorality.

UNFAITHFUL

Proverbs 6:16-19 There are six things that the Lord hates, seven that are an abomination to him: 17 haughty eyes, a lying tongue, and hands that shed innocent blood,18 a heart that devises wicked plans, feet that make haste to run to evil, 19 a false witness who breathes out lies, and one who sows discord among brothers.

Proverbs 12:19 Truthful lips endure forever, but a lying tongue is but for a moment.

Proverbs 21:6 The getting of treasures by a lying tongue is a fleeting vapor and a snare of death.

Colossians 3:9-10 Do not lie to one another, seeing that you have put off the old self[a] with its practices 10 and have put on the new self, which is being renewed in knowledge after the image of its creator.

Luke 8:17 For nothing is hidden that will not be made manifest, nor is anything secret that will not be known and come to light.

John 8:44 You are of your father the devil, and your will is to do your father's desires. He was a murderer from the beginning and does not stand in the truth because there is no truth in him. When he lies, he speaks out of his own character, for he is a liar and the father of lies.

2 Chronicles 26:16 But when he was strong, he grew proud, to his destruction. For he was unfaithful to the Lord his God and entered the temple of the Lord to burn incense on the altar of incense.

Matthew 5:27-28 You have heard that it was said, 'You shall not commit adultery.' 28 But I say to you that everyone who looks at a woman with lustful intent has already committed adultery with her in his heart.

Revelation 21:8 But as for the cowardly, the faithless, the detestable, as for murderers, the sexually immoral, sorcerers, idolaters, and all liars, their portion will be in the lake that burns with fire and sulfur, which is the second death".

1 John 2:4 Whoever says "I know him" but does not keep his commandments is a liar, and the truth is not in him,

2 Corinthians 10:4 For the weapons of our warfare are not of the flesh but have divine power to destroy strongholds.

Luke 6:45 The good person out of the good treasure of his heart produces good, and the evil person out of his evil treasure produces evil, for out of the abundance of the heart his mouth speaks.

Matthew 5:9 Blessed are the peacemakers, for they shall be called sons of God.

YOUR POWER AND FOUNDATION

If you are dealing with an unfaithful spouse, an unfaithful parent, or maybe even you being unfaithful to God or yourself, I don't want you to ignore it. We should not ignore the emotions we feel because if we think to hide them, they will come out in a way we will not be able to control. They say an honest person is a drunk because they speak their heart when they are drunk.

Out of the overflow of the heart, the mouth speaks (Luke 6:45). If you are feeling pain because

UNFAITHFUL

of something or someone who was unfaithful to you, you have to speak about this pain. We have to release this pain and allow Yah to heal us in this area. We do not want to hold on to our emotions, pinning them up, and speaking to no one, including God, about them.

He wants all of you. Not just the easy things we can talk about. Not us PGing or trying to clean up our emotions so they read better to God. He wants your raw emotion, and yes, He can handle it. Some people may not be able to, and we have to practice patience and grace. What I don't want you to do is miss out on finding someone you can share your faults with to help you heal. Don't sweep your pain under the rug.

We need to talk about the elephants in the room. We need to address the issues that have us in pain and allow ourselves to heal from them. To heal, you have to be willing to let it go. Melvina W has a book that is a bit wild, but it talks about things you need to be willing to let go of to grow. You have to be willing to admit that the pain is there. The enemy loves to hide in the dark. He loves to have you rehash the event in your heart or mind and keep you pinned in a state of constant pain. The kingdom of darkness feeds off of your pain.

When you are in pain, spirits grow stronger when you give glory to it by hiding it. By holding it from Yah or denying the pain you have to those who you need to talk about it with, you are harming yourself. I know it can be hard to have a conversation when the other party or you yourself is not ready. But something I learned, there is something we can always work on. Challenge yourself in ways you are called to grow in God.

When a person doesn't want to speak about the pain they have caused us genuinely, we often don't see how we can tame the spirit of rage working in our lives. We can make the mistake of becoming more "mean" because of what someone else has done. We can believe that this rage brewing within us is justified because of what happened. We can intentionally hold them at arm's length away because we don't trust them anymore.

How can two become one if they are permanently separated in heart, deeds, actions, love, and affection? To be married to someone is not easy; this I have learned. A marriage can only last when the two people in it are equally committed. Yes, at times one may do more, but they both must choose the relationship. If you are both willing, there is room for a breakthrough.

When we invite Yah into our painful areas, He can help us heal within ourselves, and we hold no pain against our spouse, parent, or child. Instead of rage, we feel empathy. We can see their pain even more clearly than before. We can see what evil spirit or spirits have left or the ones they are still battling.

It is in this perspective we can focus on fighting the real battle. The battle is not you versus him. You against your mother, father, children, employer, etc. It is not about you versus God. It is not even about you getting even and making them pay for the pain you feel. That won't heal you, and

UNFAITHFUL

whatever feeling you feel will be temporary.

It is about being open to healing from God and shutting down evil spirits from running your heart and mind. It is not easy to live what we believe when living as a believer brings pain. Being on the cross wasn't comfortable but brought much pain. It pained Yashua, Jesus, to feel every lash, hear every cursed word, and see every rejecting eye that watched His suffering. There are those who watched your suffering that Yah will call you to extend mercy and grace toward.

Not because of what they deserve but because of what He wants to do in you that proves what He desires for you. He says we are to prove we believe in Him by keeping His commandments (1 John 2:4). His commandment is for us to be peacekeepers and not one who stirs up strife (Matthew 5:9). The enemy loves to stir up trouble and have people act outside their character supercharging them to be angry and say malicious things.

Don't give the enemy glory by taking the bate. Those who are being tormented by pain don't always know the source of their own pain. They know they hurt, and hurt people hurt others, we often say it, and it is true. We may think there is nothing wrong with this man, woman, or child. They just choose to be unfaithful because that is who they are, we say. But if you look closer, you will see that there is a source.

When people drink, they drink because there are emotions and pains they feel that grip them, and they don't know how to release them. The only time they feel a false peace is when they drink because, for a moment, they don't remember. Although they force it out of their minds, it is not out of their hearts. They say foolish things, mean things, or truthful things when they are able to be bold and honest.

Hearing the truth can hurt. Some people will admit things we never wanted to hear, but if it is the truth, and knowing it can set you free, don't reject it. Many of us are like the young lady holding on to situations that were never meant to be. We are trying to piece bad situations back together by trying to find God in a choice that, if we were honest, He wasn't a part of from the beginning. I am not saying this is the ticket to end long-term relationships, get out of marriages, or abandon people, but the opposite. When we see the truth, we can clearly see why people are put into our lives.

People who entered my life might have been sent for ministry, and I thought something different, but God! Adam and Eve thought eating from the tree was a good idea, but it wasn't. They made a mistake, but God! He is able to turn around messy situations and give us beauty for our ashes (Isaiah 61:3). He can turn around marriages. He can restore relationships with family members and a connection within yourself or with Him.

If you need to see Him as your Healer, allow Him to be that for you. If you need Him to be your Redeemer, allow Him to redeem your heart, mind, soul, hope, future, and love. When we release the lies we have told ourselves, we can release pain, and when it leaves, the evil spirit holding on to it goes with it. It is hard for two people who are battling the same spirit to cast it out.

It takes one to get delivered and then go back to help others. We are to help and bear one another's burdens. Galatians 6:2 says, "Bear one another's burdens, and so fulfill the law of Christ." We are going to speak more about healing, but I want to spend a moment on this subject because we need to unpack the pain pointing to the stronghold of evil powers in your life.

I know, we might all get nervous when we hear evil spirits, witches, witchcraft because of movies we have seen or stories we have heard. I don't say this to scare you but to help you understand what it is you are fighting that has you feeling heavy. That has you and your family at odds. Why it seems you keep losing yourself more and more each day. How you can wake up completely lost in time, heart, and within your emotions. This is a spiritual attack, a disassociation from your true self but a shadow that hides within the tears or the blood of your pain.

You don't have to live like this. You can release this pain, and it starts by realizing the pain that has been buried, hidden, or denied. When we expose our truth, we can deal with it. When we expose what hurts us to Yah and give Him authority over the area, we are now truly in the fight. Some battles are short, and others require prayer and fasting. Some will need you to tarry in prayer or to stay to be the light.

It is not easy to remain in place when you feel abused, misused, or that others are doing less than you. We can feel like Martha and ask Jesus to make others match our output. The truth, not everyone will–but God will always outdo you! He will always pay for those who have no money, no shame, no regrets for what they have done. Allow His grace and mercy to bring you strength as you journey on this path of deliverance. It is not a one-and-done, although you can be made light right now, to keep this deliverance, you want to practice deliverance.

Let's keep journeying.

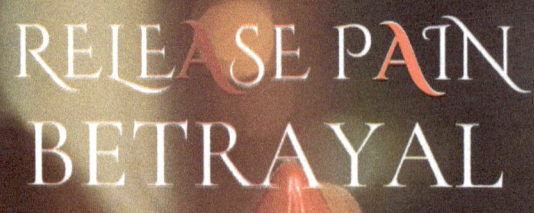

BETRAYAL

Nothing can stab deeper than betrayal. I know it hurts to have someone you love and care for do you dirty. We all can relate to the Messiah and how He had to deal with unfaithful friends, followers, and people. I heard a saying that will always be with me, "That person, there is a snake in the grass." When I first heard it, I didn't know what it meant.

I quickly learned, as I watched the person he spoke about, that the snake is an individual who is watching you not to learn but to find your weaknesses. This person is an opportunist, and they can masquerade as a friend although they are a foe. Another name is Frienemie. Someone who today might be your friend, but the moment they can burn the bridge for something that benefits them, they won't hesitate to throw you under the bus.

People like this are the friends who try to create limiting thoughts and not expose their hand. They will see you happy and try to "bring you back to reality." You will get a break, and they will remind you to be cautious and not trust it. They will talk you into doubting yourself and what you think. They hope to have a voice that is louder in your head than your voice or the Word of God.

RELEASE PAIN

When you see someone who can never be happy for you–even when the setting is all the way right, know you might have a snake in the grass. Having friends like this could make anyone cautious about making new ones and sharing the pain you are doing the work to release. It can be scary to meet new people when you are working on trust, and these people show up.

But these people are on assignment from the devil to be a distraction, a stumbling block to your progress. Don't be surprised when they show up and don't feel you have to kick them out of your life so quickly. In that, the Father could use you to show them the way to the Truth. Many witches and wizards are converted by believers every day. With love and kindness, we can draw people back to Yah, and that is a victory for the Kingdom of God (Jeremiah 31:2-4).

It is a sad phenomenon and belief that a lot of believers think they can live their lives void of spiritual warfare. That we can essentially obtain all this Word, sharing and showing the light, and no threat will come our way to get us to stop converting and winning souls. This is not an Easter egg hunt where everyone is happy to be found. People are mad. The kingdom of darkness is upset with you because you are helping to set the captives free!

Like in jail or prison, the prison complex doesn't rejoice when people get out and stay out. They don't make money if people are not working for pennies or twenty-five cent on the dollar. This system is fed people, and it chews up dreams, hopes, and plans. It loves to crush and destroy, but Yah can take this solitude and work something great. The life story of Stephan Barbee is an incredible read for those who are restarting their journey after incarceration.

BETRAYAL

He was gifted from the beginning, coming from a family that is strong in pastoral leadership and ministry. He was called, but he didn't want to serve. He wanted to live the life in his head and heart, but not in his reality and that choice had consequences. The fleeting happiness he received from a life of sin was great for the season. But the high he got quickly sobered him when he was called to serve a long sentence.

The high we get from doing evil will betray us once it destroys our lives, and this is why we must not give up on living a righteous life. Why we must watch our friends and the company we keep. Even why we should ask the tough questions before we live the outcome of being silent.

So what makes a friend determined to commit the ultimate betrayal? What makes people plot to do injustice against another person? What makes them think they deserve something so much that they can steal or take it from someone else? It is hurtful and cruel to take what you have not earned, especially when it comes from loved ones and people who need it.

I have seen people steal from others who didn't have much. Like Uriah, King David stole the only thing he had of value. Remember the play that was popular and redone, "A Raisin in the Sun?" This play was so powerful because the family had money and could have survived, but the son thought his dream was more important than the family's survival.

He didn't host a meeting on how to invest the insurance money. He went to a friend, supposed friend, who didn't regard the money in the same way. He saw him as an easy mark, an easy person to talk into a joint venture that he had already planned would fail. He knew he had a backup plan to leave with money no matter the outcome.

When we throw good money after bad ideas, we find that we can lose out. I love that the title has "raisin" and "sun." A healthy grape is luscious, seeded, juicy, and full of nutrition. Our dreams are wide open and full of hope. We are plentiful. When they had the insurance money, their dreams could expand, and they could dream again. What was limited by their resources was unleashed.

The family had hope, and then, with a decision, that hope was stolen. It hurt the family when the son made his choice. He betrayed their confidence and dismissed their plans, hopes, and dreams. His mother, who slaved to earn a roof over his head, he didn't even consult with her about his choice. She was calmer than most of us in that she didn't try to fight him, slap him, or threaten him like others wanted to.

I think in some of our lives, if we came into a large amount of money and one of the relatives blew it for everyone, there would be at least one fistfight. I know the believers wouldn't be fighting, just the ones who are still worldly and all. Smile. Some of us would "lose our salvation" for about 20 minutes while we beat that person down for costing us the huge penalty of not being able to achieve our version of good. We would be mad that they kept us back from "being great."

It hurts our families when one person decides to betray the family. One narcissist can do a whole lot of damage. I heard a statistic that says people today who are mostly concerned about self-care and self-preservation are sicker today than when we had to be a unit and live as a family about 50 years ago. You would think with all this technology and presumed growth, the quality of life would increase.

After looking around more, we find that the only things that have increased are poison in foods, waistlines, and sickness. Most families today can barely speak with each other, and I am talking about parents and children. Strokes, a stress-induced response, are going up, and the age of stroke victims is going down.

When one partner thinks for themselves and not the whole, the marriage breaks down, and the union that was full of hope and promise is deteriorating. Turning something great into something that you have to claw to get out of is not God's design. Relationships, unions, and marriage are for the betterment of both and all parties. We are to become better, stronger because of unity and not self-destruction.

I know the regret had to be brutal on his heart to be the one responsible for washing away everyone's dreams. I am sure he got the dirty looks at family events, and people didn't want to speak to him. I imagine some wanted to kill him, not because of the money, in my opinion, but because they are back to where they started.

Have you ever made progress, and something or someone took you back to start? I hate playing Monopoly and Trouble because I don't like going backward. You work hard, pressing your fingers on the pop ball with just enough pressure to illuminate the white skin underneath to get a "6" to get out. Only to be landed on a few spots away from home and sent back.

When it happens, you have to look up and breathe out. Remember that this game is not personal, even though it feels like a plastic knife sawing at your hands. It is annoying, and you want the pain to end, ideally to win, but after going home enough times, you just want the bleeding to stop.

"Oh, maybe it is just me? Don't pay me no mind." I like Phase Ten, but I hardly ever play Uno because I don't like how that game makes my stomach tie up in knots. How can you start off with a good hand, and a few moves later, you are stuck with a thick fan big enough to slap somebody, and it hurts?

I am not violent, but that game brings out too much anxiety for my liking. Maybe I am too competitive? My momma and daughter, Zoe, play until tears roll. I know when to gracefully bow out, but my momma has no surrender, and neither does Zoe.

It can hurt us to start on a path and begin to make progress only to repeat the steps back at one. This is not a cute back-to-one like Bryan McKnight sings, this feels more like forty years in the wilderness! As you start seeing the light at the end of the tunnel, that's when it happens. You are flung backward by a job loss, loss of income, someone leaves, an employee quits, or you lose a big client. Now, what was working smoothly is bumpy yet again, and like being in quicksand, your feet feel as heavy as your heart.

Nothing can prepare you for losing something you thought was in the bag. When you get your family on point, and your child is the one that steals a car, robs a store, or does something foolish. They betray you by not listening to your sound advice and instead choosing to do their own thing. When people are focused on themselves, selfishness will cause them to betray others and find a way to rationalize it.

A narcissist is something we are all growing

BETRAYAL

more familiar with every day. This is now almost a pop culture saying because of how frequently the word is used. I think we can use it as a go-to for describing many people because our society prides itself on achieving what we want by any means. Some people will slap their momma for a million dollars. There is no limit to what we will do, and we have lost honor in our pursuit of riches and things.

What is it that we desire that would have us turn on our family? The hurt of someone you love betraying you for favorable circumstances or people is hard to bear. Psalm 55:12-14 says, "For it is not an enemy who taunts me—then I could bear it; it is not an adversary who deals insolently with me—then I could hide from him. 13 But it is you, a man, my equal, my companion, my familiar friend. 14 We used to take sweet counsel together; within God's house, we walked in the throng."

It is not our enemies that cause the most damage from betrayal but our family. Those who come and sleep on your couch, you have helped in their time of need, or you willingly helped out of the goodness of your heart. When these people take your gifts but deny you the reciprocal treatment, it is betrayal. It is a slap in the face that stings.

It is hard to understand why someone who you talked to and shared things about you in confidence would want to betray your trust. It could be understandable if someone betrayed you to protect the greater good, but how many have been betrayed for no good reason? For gossip and to be something to talk about is how many of us fill out a person's conversation. Are people not more than hot topics and modes for some people to be a busybody?

In Genesis 37:18-28 the Bible reports the plans of Joseph's brothers. "They saw him from afar, and before he came near to them, they conspired against him to kill him. 19 They said to one another, "Here comes this dreamer.

20 Come now, let us kill him and throw him into one of the pits. Then we will say that a fierce animal has devoured him, and we will see what will become of his dreams." 21 But when Reuben heard it, he rescued him out of their hands, saying, "Let us not take his life."

22 And Reuben said to them, "Shed no blood; throw him into this pit here in the wilderness, but do not lay a hand on him"—that he might rescue him out of their hand to restore him to his father. 23 So when Joseph came to his brothers, they stripped him of his robe, the robe of many colors that he wore. 24 And they took him and threw him into a pit. The pit was empty; there was no water in it.

25 Then they sat down to eat. And looking up, they saw a caravan of Ishmaelites coming from Gilead, with their camels bearing gum, balm, and myrrh, on their way to carry it down to Egypt. 26 Then Judah said to his brothers, "What profit is it if we kill our brother and conceal his blood?

27 Come, let us sell him to the Ishmaelites, and let not our hand be upon him, for he is our brother, our own flesh." And his brothers listened to him. 28 Then Midianite traders passed by. And they drew Joseph up and lifted him out of the pit, and sold him to the Ishmaelites for twenty shekels of silver. They took Joseph to Egypt."

Nothing could describe the gut-wrenching feeling he felt. Nothing could have dwarfed the pain of betrayal more than the sadness he may have felt to be disowned and sold by his own! I know many sold in slavery felt a similar way when they looked up and saw people who looked like them selling

BETRAYAL

them for trinkets and things. Those who were jealous of you thought of selling you to remove you from your blessing.

Some plans plotted to betray you are not because of something you have done to deserve it. Are you perfect? No, no one is. But that doesn't mean we deserve the betrayal we all receive. Jeremiah 9:4 says, "Let everyone beware of his neighbor, and put no trust in any brother, for every brother is a deceiver, and every neighbor goes about as a slanderer."

When we are in a hostile environment, it can be hard to trust anyone. We are not to glorify anyone because anybody can turn their back on us. Our truest confidence should be in the Lord alone. We can love and expect the best, but our hope should remain in Yah alone. Anyone can hurt our hearts, and they will. They can say something or do something that will require grace and mercy for us to forgive.

We are to forgive because we, too, can expect and receive forgiveness when we forgive others. "For if you forgive others their trespasses, your heavenly Father will also forgive you, 15 but if you do not forgive others their trespasses, neither will your Father forgive your trespasses (Matthew 6:14-15)." Even though it hurts to forgive people for their betrayal, it is in our best interest to release the pain. We cannot hold others hostage for their mistakes to our own detriment.

I know it is easier said than done. We are all human, and it can be tempting to think, who can get past this? Who can forgive? Some would argue that no one is able to deny their own desires but will cave at some point to their own lusts.

We can have confidence in overcoming betrayal because our Advocate, the Holy One, Yashua the Christ, can relate to how we feel. He knows what it is like to lose a friend for no good reason. He knows what it is like to have His friends betray or abandon Him and sell Him out for money.

Hebrews 4:15 says, "For we do not have a high priest who is unable to sympathize with our weaknesses, but one who in every respect has been tempted as we are, yet without sin"

If those who ate with the Bread of Life could find a justified reason to betray Him, how can we not expect that those we love could not do the same? "John 13:18 writes, "I am not speaking of all of you; I know whom I have chosen. But the Scripture will be fulfilled, 'He who ate my bread has lifted his heel against me." What a heartbreak and lonely place to be. Judas had no rest after betraying Christ. He was tormented, and the reason that seemed good enough to betray the Messiah was no longer something he wanted.

How many have lost families and friends because they accepted far less than the value of what they had in the guise of being happier? The enemy's trick is to tell us we will be better off if only we ditched this dead weight. The issue is not in losing weight but how you move away from people. It is not right to use and abuse people, and in the same way, Judas had no rest from doing ultimately, God, the one who sent Yashau dirty.

Those who thought it was a good deal to betray their family and friends for money, status, accomplishments, homes, etc, soon find out it is lonely at the top. The way to become isolated is to choose to separate yourself from those that love and work to protect you. The enemy's plan is to get us all alone, so we listen to him and lean on our own understanding.

BETRAYAL

Judas didn't know what to do after offending Yah. He tried to give the money back and was denied. Matthew 27:3-4 records, "When Judas, who had betrayed him, saw that Jesus was condemned, he was seized with remorse and returned the thirty pieces of silver to the chief priests and the elders. 4 "I have sinned," he said, "for I have betrayed innocent blood." "What is that to us?" they replied. "That's your responsibility." Ain't it funny how those who helped you make poor decisions are not around when the penalty comes?

The many friends you had now hate you or deny your friendship openly. Job 19:19 says, "All my intimate friends abhor me, and those whom I loved have turned against me. The many who make the news for criminal activities or doing stuff they ain't got no business, when they are blasted, those who were close start shifting farther and farther away. Their name is run through the mud, and those who they called friends they quickly find were no friends at all. "For even your brothers and the house of your father, even they have dealt treacherously with you; they are in full cry after you; do not believe them, though they speak friendly words to you" (Jeremiah 12:6).

Anyone who tries to get you to do something to your own hurt, even if the feeling might be enjoyable for a season, has treacherous plans for you and your life. Although their words appear friendly, don't believe it. So many step out of their marriages and forget about their responsibilities because of the people in their ears. They will tell you a little sin won't hurt. Doing this one time won't cost your marriage. But it only takes one Big Mistake, to lose everything!

Obadiah 1:7 reads, "All your allies have driven you to your border; those at peace with you have deceived you; they have prevailed against you;

those who eat your bread have set a trap beneath you—you have no understanding." For those who sleep around on their wives, it seems like the side piece was waiting or even hoping to get pregnant. Some see the success of others as a means to get in and steal. They are not loyal, and soon after they betray one person, another betrays them. There is no loyalty among thieves.

It is bewildering to see how quickly the tables turn against those guilty of betraying another. Judas had plans to spend the money he got. Yet, the demons that come with betrayal came to live with him. He was driven insane and ended up taking his own life. Before things get that tough, we are better off denying ourselves. We are better to go and seek forgiveness than to allow the demon of torment and betrayal to take root in our lives.

King David prayed that the whispers of a close friend to his son would be ignored and turned to foolishness concerning the throne. 2 Samuel 15:31 records, "And it was told David, "Ahithophel is among the conspirators with Absalom." And David said, "O Lord, please turn the counsel of Ahithophel into foolishness."

A conversation that should have been a non-issue became the plan of a trap to take the kingdom away from King David. His son tried to kill him and take the kingdom, but he would never inherit it. The Kingdom was not promised to him,

BETRAYAL

and he should have known better, but greed and pride blinded him.

Those who think of betraying you and stealing what is yours, too, will find they cannot take what belongs to you! What the Father has for you is for you. The plans the enemy whispers into people's ears you love, He will come against. He knows the plans He has for you, and they are to bless you and bring you an expected end. If we ever find ourselves on the outside of the will of Yah, we must recenter our lives.

When we are betrayed, it is normal to cry and acknowledge the pain in our hearts and if there are limitations in our minds. "She weeps bitterly in the night, with tears on her cheeks; among all her lovers she has none to comfort her; all her friends have dealt treacherously with her; they have become her enemies" (Lamentations 1:2). We are human, and work to keep a heart of flesh so that those who deserve to be let into our hearts can have access. The hurt of betrayal threatens our ability to love and receive love.

The deepest wounds we carry are the ones in our back. The knives in our back are usually from those within our homes. I love the verse, and yet I find so much pain in Zechariah 13:6. "And if one asks him, 'What are these wounds on your back?' He will say, 'The wounds I received in the house of my friends.'" You open your arms to your friends, children, and family. You allow them into your intimate space, and for them to use you or turn to stab you in the back hurts.

I know it hurt King David to hear his son was killed in his attempt to take the throne. I am sure if his son came to him with a knife, he wouldn't have defended himself to the point he would killed his son. He would have permitted his own death before allowing that to happen. We can feel as if we have no defense, but we have One who knows the beginning and the end and He fights for you.

He knows how to treat others, and He plans to avenge you, especially if you have no plans to do it yourself. No sin will go unaccounted for. Either the blood of the lamb will cover the sin, or the person will pay for it.

Psalms 41:9-10: Even my close friend in whom I trusted, who ate my bread, has lifted his heel against me. 10 But you, O Lord, be gracious to me, and raise me up, that I may repay them! The Father is gracious, and He will help us to keep our hearts pure so that we may repay evil with Good! We can think if we have been wronged, we deserve to treat them like the thieves, adulterers, and ungrateful children they are. But like King David, we pray their plans come to foolishness! We pray that our plans to avenge ourselves in any other way that doesn't honor Yah be canceled. It is written, "If anyone returns evil for good, evil will not depart from his house" (Proverbs 17:13).

When we seek out our own vengeance and return evil for evil, we will always deal with the demon of betrayal. You will not send this evil spirit packing if you are willing to embrace the evil thoughts it sends as a solution to your pain. When we have unresolved pain and have not dealt with the issue of our betrayal, it will chew at us. This demon will wake you up and have you replay the incident over and over in your head, trying to figure it out.

Only you will never figure it out. Betrayal is the evidence of sin when we do what we don't want to do, but we do it because we are not stronger than the temptation (Romans 7:15-20). "For I do not

BETRAYAL

understand my own actions. For I do not do what I want, but I do the very thing I hate. 16 Now, if I do what I do not want, I agree with the law that it is good. 17 So now it is no longer I who do it, but sin that dwells within me."

Not everyone who betrays their own heart does it intentionally–in that they intend to hurt themselves. It is the sin that lies within them that makes this decision to sin and follow through with the action. It is a battle that the host is losing.

When we are not mature enough to deny what can bring joy for a season, we put our happiness and life at risk. We will lose the greater chasing a fleeting emotion or physical addiction. We can look at those who throw their lives away for a prostitute, a liar, or a fling and question their intellect. But it is their sinful nature that should be on trial.

When sin has a grip on your soul, it can confound you in what you would do. You are not rational, thinking through the details, but your sinful nature has taken the lead, and your body is aimlessly following along for the ride, trying to get a glimpse of fulfillment if it can be obtained. This is probably the worst time to have bad sex when it costs you everything.

As I write this section, I must confess that betrayal, to any degree, sucks. I remember when I met a man who appeared to be in a good place in his life. He was hurting when I met him, I soon learned, but against my better judgment, I gave him a shot. We met on an online platform, something I am not the most supportive of. With catfishing being more popular nowadays than reality, I wasn't interested in internet dating.

I was having a conversation with a friend of mine, exchanging catfish stories recently. I think his catfish took the cake over mine! He said that his story was worse, and I questioned how. I mean, one lie isn't that much greater than another, I thought. It is a fib to say they were taller, skinnier, muscular, etc. No big deal, but it is a red flag. They're either in denial, struggling with self-image, or they are so used to telling a lie that they don't notice the problem.

He told me he had been talking to a woman for several weeks before he agreed to meet her. When he did, he knew the woman–was a man! I said, "Whoa! Yeah, you got me. I have never been catfished like that." That is the worst kind of betrayal. To tell someone you are something you are not, a woman when you are a born man. Needless to say, he has been single for the last 7 years and is content with waiting for Mrs. Right. I have no doubt she is coming his way.

I wasn't catfished on this date, and he looked like his picture, but I don't think he was honest about his initial intent. I was told to try dating him because I was "too young" to be single. I have heard, "Your children need a father, Krystal," and as soon as it was said, I cringed. I haven't had the best of luck when it comes to dating.

Life is far more simple when I stay in the lane of being single. Perhaps it is because I am aware of what can happen in the circle of those who should love you. I try not to be bitter about life, and I am not, but on the other hand, I don't have the mushy ideals of marriage and relationships.

I want things to be different from my previous marriages. I am willing to wait to find it–even more so now than before. I had hopes for this guy being different from my past relationships and thought putting my honest heart forward would be the right thing to do. It wasn't, haha. My first mind told me not to go, and when I saw him, I heard it again. I will tell you why in a minute. But after speaking a bit, he texted me, and I reluctantly agreed to meet him. I arrived early, got my chai tea, and sat there waiting. He wasn't too late and was pleasant.

What I noticed immediately was that he was wearing the same shoes and jacket as an 'ex' of mine. That should have been a good enough red flag, but I moved past it. I thought the conversation would be quick, but we chatted for about two hours, and the time blew by. We agreed that even if we weren't to date romantically, we would be friends. Oh Boy, if I were the wishing type, I would have wished we remained friends from the start. We are on agreeable and speaking terms even now and respect each other's business and accomplishments, but it was a rabbit chase romantically.

We hung out a few days later, and it was a good time, too. It seemed like in a week, he grew attached and told me he loved me. I laughed and thought he was joking, but he got upset with my response. So, I steered clear of the conversation after that. I wasn't in love and questioned if I ever was. I did have a respect for him, but I think knowing we wouldn't work out dulled any strong emotions over the next year and a half. We didn't have the same love for God, music, or entertainment.

But the real reason we would grow to become nothing was because I questioned his ability to move forward with a new relationship with his open doors. He was going through a legal dispute when we started talking and was uncertain of the outcome. I prayed with him and over him and shared what I saw. Unfortunately, I also saw that he would return to the woman who caused the legal cloud in his life.

I told him, "She isn't done. She will be back." He laughed and said, "How do you know?" I replied, "If you go back, it won't be like how you think." I said more, but I knew it would cost him. He said he wasn't going back and he wanted to be with me. A part of me wanted to believe this could be the one that would last. We had fun in his city when we were sightseeing, but I wasn't a fan of nightclubs and things. So that was another red flag. I felt displaced when I was in his city.

Have you ever longed to be in a place familiar to you? You weren't having a bad time. You just knew you were in the wrong place? I felt that way, but I still wanted to do my best. I cooked, encouraged him, heard him speak of his past relationships, and even encouraged him to pursue where his heart was. I knew the relationship was shifting to friendship, but when I got a text message from his ex-girlfriend talking about my life, I knew he had said too much about me to a stranger.

When he wanted to hang out with me, I found out he had recently been with her. He was a mess, and although he might have had the makings of a good husband with his financial, easy conversation, wisdom, good looks, humor, and fathering skills. It was lacking the commitment and integrity I needed. I knew he would not likely be with me, but I wasn't expecting him to betray my confidence and share things about me with his exes. I guess I was naive, and I hated that I had invested in another relationship that quickly, within a two-year span, came to nothing.

After this relationship, I wasn't heartbroken but disappointed, not in him but in myself. I wanted nothing to do with a relationship, and I think some of that still remains as I write this book. I am content with being single because I think my view on marriage needs to be healed. I haven't picked relationships that were healthy or lasted. Most of my relationships take years, and the divorce process takes three years. Going through that twice, I am so good on starting over.

I want to learn more and practice what I preach to find me and what I honestly need from a husband. I was asked that question, and I could not answer it. A lot of what I need I have in Yah, my children, business, friendships, ministry, hobbies, and sleep. I just don't have time right now, and I am okay with that. I also don't want to feed a negative taste that was in my mouth from my past relationships ending because of unfaithfulness, cheating, and lack of commitment on their part. I have to release any lingering pain so when Mr. Right does come, I will be ready.

I don't hate marriage, but I can relate to those who are afraid to trust their own judgment. I felt like I betrayed myself by dating a person like this for nearly two years. I was taking it seriously, but perhaps not serious enough.

He asked me to marry him once over the phone, and I told him I would believe him when he gave me the ring to match the words. He never did, so I knew it was air. I am glad I didn't laugh on the phone. I think that would have made things awkward. My heart knew it was a joke, but I did want to believe it for a moment.

I think that also exposed something about me and my thinking. I realized although I say "yeah," I will get married someday...again. A part of me is not looking for it at all. I have grown content with being single, and it seems like when I am the most content, someone prophesies or says something about the right man coming. I am not too sure about that, but know I have had to release pain from my own betrayal.

I have said the things I wanted in a marriage, but I consistently picked men who didn't meet the standard. I thought I was being reasonable, but I felt that I was living beneath my expectations because I thought I could be asking for too much, and then I realized it wasn't enough. It's a conundrum; don't pay me any mind. I am sure for you, some things are still a work in progress to resolve the conflict within your heart and mind. That's okay, too. We are growing together. This is why I started the "Growing Book Club."

Now, I am in a happy wait period with no clock, and I have silenced all the noise. I enjoy my children, my business, my ministry, and my life. I don't see it as robbery for me to be happy with where I am, and I have learned to bring my own joy. I can go to the gym, watch movies, or eat dinner alone, and it feels like a treat! Others still say, "God is not done with you. All you do for Him, He is going to send you a husband."

I am thankful for the words, but I mute the statement to stay focused on what's in front of me. Their words in my heart are like getting a bouquet of flowers I put on the table to look at and call beautiful. I admire the sentiment, but most of my work is done away from the table, and it cannot rule my heart or expectations.

Ironically, that guy and I can still work together to help people start their businesses and

BETRAYAL

achieve personal goals. Some people can struggle in one area with you but work in another. I had to learn that everyone in my life who enters one way doesn't have to stay in that position. When we met, I wished I would have seen him as a ministry case and not a romantic one. A business connection and not a love match.

I cannot blame him for the imbalance I went through in those roughly two years. We can learn things about ourselves through betrayal. I saw his betrayal and was hurt, but it took me longer to acknowledge my betrayal. Involving myself in activities I had no business and playing house was something I did against Yah. I repented for my part in my own pain.

I realized I was like Peter in denying Christ and His ability to provide what I desired. I was settling for what I thought would be good enough, and I missed every time. I had faith to get me through my decision, but I did not have enough courage or conviction to call a spade a spade.

Some people will not be good enough. Some people who want to date you or get close to you can have what you need on your list but miss the fundamental requirements. I desire a husband who has a heart for Yah and is on a level with God higher or equal to where I am. Not someone who can just say they believe in God, but one who lives the Word of Yah. I need more than nice cars, a fancy house, money in the bank, good looks, or even great sex.

I am being even more patient and working to silence all voices that rise against the Word for my life. We are not too old, and we are not too late to get it right. We can have expectations for our lives and standards. In one of the last conversations I had with the guy, I told him, "I will find the right guy one day and will get married to someone who

RELEASE PAIN

treats me better than you did." We both laughed, and he said, "I hear you. You deserve it."

Sometimes, that is the best people who hurt you can offer you. To touch and agree to what you want for yourself. Release the pain and any malice you hold in your heart against someone. When we realize that the one we thought got away was never meant to be that for us, we can be free to embrace the right person, circumstance, or dreams.

Whatever the Father has for you, He is able to fulfill, and sometimes the fulfillment comes at the expense of moving others out of your life. We can shed a tear and pray for them but don't allow betrayal to keep you away from what is yours. Or if you have betrayed God with choices you have made, don't run away from Him.

Don't think it is too late, too dirty or not good enough to visit the Throne of Grace. He is able to clean you and make you as white as snow. He can remove all pain, malice in your heart, or fear stored in your memory. He can help you move on with confidence and not run to another situation familiar to your past. He can break the unholy bond between you and familiar spirits.

Familiar spirits want to keep us in a familiar life pattern that ends in heartbreak. We are stronger and much wiser than before when we make the Word the foundation of our lives. The pain is what fuels the enemy's camp and brings them glory. But if we release it, they have nothing to hold on to because your joy they cannot hold. We can overcome betrayal because we realize the people who have left us or that we have left were not meant to be in this part of our lives. Everything we must endure will work to our good, even if it is our fault for the break.

There is redemption in Yah that gives you a

light heart and a clean conscience. When we Embrace Our Crown, purpose, and life's calling, we will release the pain and make life changes to maintain it. You can overcome Heartbreak and Unbelief by Sharpening your Focus on being delivered.

Don't allow people, specifically demons or evil spirits, to hold you in mental or emotional jail for your past. All sins are forgiven (Mark 3:28). The old has gone, and the new has come (2 Corinthians 5:17). If you desire marriage, our God is able to give it to you. Is anything too wonderful or difficult for God (Genesis 18:14)?

He wants to give you beauty for ashes and hope where there wasn't none (Isaiah 61:3).

EMPOWERING SCRIPTURES: INJUSTICE

Genesis 18:14 Is anything too hard[a] for the Lord? At the appointed time, I will return to you, about this time next year, and Sarah shall have a son."

2 Corinthians 5:17 Therefore, if anyone is in Christ, he is a new creation. The old has passed away; behold, the new has come.

Mark 3:28 Truly, I say to you, all sins will be forgiven the children of man, and whatever blasphemies they utter,

Romans 7:15-17 For I do not understand my own actions. For I do not do what I want, but I do the very thing I hate. 16 Now, if I do what I do not want, I agree with the law that it is good. 17 So now it is no longer I who do it, but sin that dwells within me.

Hebrews 4:15 "For we do not have a high priest who is unable to sympathize with our weaknesses, but one who in every respect has been tempted as we are, yet without sin"

Matthew 6:14-15 For if you forgive others their trespasses, your heavenly Father will also forgive you, 15 but if you do not forgive others their trespasses, neither will your Father forgive your trespasses.

Matthew 27:3-4 When Judas, who had betrayed him, saw that Jesus was condemned, he was seized with remorse and returned the thirty pieces of silver to the chief priests and the elders. 4 "I have sinned," he said, "for I have betrayed innocent blood." "What is that to us?" they replied. "That's your responsibility."

Hebrews 4:15 "For we do not have a high priest who is unable to sympathize with our weaknesses, but one who in every respect has been tempted as we are, yet without sin"

2 Samuel 15:31 And it was told David, "Ahithophel is among the conspirators with Absalom." And David said, "O Lord, please turn the counsel of Ahithophel into foolishness."

BETRAYAL

John 13:18 I am not speaking of all of you; I know whom I have chosen. But the Scripture will be fulfilled, 'He who ate my bread has lifted his heel against me.'

Obadiah 1:7 All your allies have driven you to your border; those at peace with you have deceived you; they have prevailed against you; those who eat your bread[a] have set a trap beneath you—you have no understanding.

Job 19:19 All my intimate friends abhor me, and those whom I loved have turned against me.

Jeremiah 9:4 Let everyone beware of his neighbor, and put no trust in any brother, for every brother is a deceiver, and every neighbor goes about as a slanderer.

Lamentations 1:2 She weeps bitterly in the night, with tears on her cheeks; among all her lovers she has none to comfort her; all her friends have dealt treacherously with her; they have become her enemies.

Psalms 55:12-14 For it is not an enemy who taunts me—then I could bear it; it is not an adversary who deals insolently with me—then I could hide from him. 13 But it is you, a man, my equal, my companion, my familiar friend. 14 We used to take sweet counsel together; within God's house we walked in the throng.

Proverbs 25:9-10 Argue your case with your neighbor himself and do not reveal another's secret, 10 lest he who hears you bring shame upon you, and your ill repute have no end.

Psalms 41:9-10 Even my close friend in whom I trusted, who ate my bread, has lifted his heel against me. 10 But you, O Lord, be gracious to me, and raise me up, that I may repay them!

Proverbs 17:13 If anyone returns evil for good, evil will not depart from his house.

Micah 7:5-6 Put no trust in a neighbor; have no confidence in a friend; guard the doors of your mouth from her who lies in your arms;[a] 6 for the son treats the father with contempt, the daughter rises up against her mother, the daughter-in-law against her mother-in-law; a man's enemies are the men of his own house.

Jeremiah 12:6 For even your brothers and the house of your father, even they have dealt treacherously with you; they are in full cry after you; do not believe them, though they speak friendly words to you."

Genesis 37:18-28 They saw him from afar, and before he came near to them, they conspired against him to kill him. 19 They said to one another, "Here comes this dreamer. 20 Come now, let us kill him and throw him into one of the pits. Then we will say that a fierce animal has devoured him, and we will see what will become of his dreams."

21 But when Reuben heard it, he rescued him out of their hands, saying, "Let us not take his life." 22 And Reuben said to them, "Shed no blood; throw him into this pit here in the wilderness, but do not lay a hand on him"—that he might rescue him out of their hand to restore him to his father. 23 So when Joseph came to his brothers, they stripped him of his robe, the robe of many colors that he wore.

24 And they took him and threw him into a pit. The pit was empty; there was no water in it. 25 Then they sat down to eat. And looking up they saw a caravan of Ishmaelites coming from Gilead, with their camels bearing gum, balm, and myrrh, on

BETRAYAL

their way to carry it down to Egypt.

26 Then Judah said to his brothers, "What profit is it if we kill our brother and conceal his blood? 27 Come, let us sell him to the Ishmaelites, and let not our hand be upon him, for he is our brother, our own flesh." And his brothers listened to him. 28 Then Midianite traders passed by. And they drew Joseph up and lifted him out of the pit, and sold him to the Ishmaelites for twenty shekels[b] of silver. They took Joseph to Egypt.

Zechariah 13:6 And if one asks him, 'What are these wounds on your back?'[a] he will say, 'The wounds I received in the house of my friends.'

Romans 5:8 but God shows his love for us in that while we were still sinners, Christ died for us.

Matthew 26:34 Jesus said to him, "Truly, I tell you, this very night, before the rooster crows, you will deny me three times."

Matthew 26:47-49 While he was still speaking, Judas came, one of the twelve, and with him a great crowd with swords and clubs, from the chief priests and the elders of the people. 48 Now, the betrayer had given them a sign, saying, "The one I will kiss is the man; seize him." 49 And he came up to Jesus at once and said, "Greetings, Rabbi!" And he kissed him.

2 Corinthians 11:14-15 And no wonder, for even Satan disguises himself as an angel of light. 15 So it is no surprise if his servants, also disguise themselves as servants of righteousness. Their end will correspond to their deeds.

YOUR POWER AND FOUNDATION

Proverbs 25:9-10 Argue your case with your neighbor himself and do not reveal another's secret, 10 lest he who hears you bring shame upon you, and your ill repute have no end.

Have you ever said something accidentally that you regretted? Sometimes, we don't intentionally seek to betray a friend, but it comes out by accident. We can think to defend our innocents so much that we offer information that doesn't be long to us. We can share details about someone else and uncover their secrets.

We have all watched movies where a character is busted for something. They then look around the room to the judgment of others, and they feel the need to plead their case. They try to explain that it is not only them who have flaws but everyone in the room. The spotlight on their mistakes is making the room hot. Out of a desperate attempt to shift the laser on their life, they begin to share the secrets of others.

If you have seen the movie by Tyler Perry, "Why Did I Get Married," the first one. The husband, who was treating his wife crappy, ultimately decided to leave her for her friend, who he had been cheating on her with. At the dinner table where the affair was revealed, he went one by one, sharing the secrets of others. This rocked the foundation of the presumed healthy relationships, and everyone left the table upset. Someone was even hit in the head with a bottle of wine that cut the scene!

BETRAYAL

Like this man, people can blurt out how others were cheating on their spouse, too. Or making life choices and not telling the other person, lying, and even blaming someone for something that they say they have forgiven. Betrayal can cut through us sometimes like a knife. It can leave any of us at a loss for words, dumbfounded and devastated. Although the person who had the spotlight on them initially may have shifted the laser from their direction, they did not change their guilt. We can think that by sharing others' stories, we are making our situation better, but we are not.

When we run from the correction that is ours, we delay our own timing. We cannot escape the correction that is meant for us by deflecting. Distractions only delay what is to come but they don't change the details. If you wronged someone, you will want to address it and the sooner the better.

Running from fixing the problems we create doesn't make us brave or thoughtful. It is the opposite. It is selfish and unfair. Taking responsibility is a cornerstone of maturity and strength. Being able to admit your mistakes proves humility. Blaming others for your mistakes in your heart or out loud will hold you in your own delusion.

For those of us who have been betrayed, know that those who have hurt us and have not admitted or taken accountability, we can pray for them as we pray for ourselves. Not so that we give them more of us but so we can release our pain. A true sign that you have been healed is when you can honestly pray for those who have hurt you. Betrayal is deep, but while we were still sinners, Yashua died on the cross for our sins (Romans 5:8).

The ones who were responsible for His death, He was still moved to intercede for them on the cross. He is our example of how to grow and live on despite betrayal. Those who can be open to empathizing with the suffering of others are able to have deep relationships.

Words can be a mask to hide true intentions when the actions of a person does not match. To learn from our own past hurts is a good thing. We all can think more highly of ourselves than we should. We can overlook our faults because we are praying for better. There is nothing wrong with growth, but don't fall in love with potential. Fall in love with who they are and be patient to allow them to grow into who they will become. Don't bypass the red or caution flags you see in someone's behaviors.

Be honest about what you are looking for and who. Not everyone is driven by love, but some are led by a need to control others through their emotions. Anyone who wants you to lower your standards for success and happiness, don't allow those people to break you down. On your job, some would try to convince you that a little trouble is no big deal. However, compromising your values weakens your ability to make sound and good decisions.

Betrayal can come from all directions, including business, family, romantic relations, and so forth. We must choose to distance ourselves from toxic people and those who seek to corrupt our values. If you see the signs of people wanting to have you live beneath your authority in Christ, deny their teaching and artificial love. Be careful about what you entertain in your heart and mind.

Betrayal hurts so much because it doesn't appear to be evil at the onset but can be charming and sensible. But remember the snake, the devil, tries to appear as an angel of light, but the end

BETRAYAL

leads to darkness (2 Corinthians 11:14-15). "And no wonder, for even Satan disguises himself as an angel of light. 15 So it is no surprise if his servants also, disguise themselves as servants of righteousness. Their end will correspond to their deeds." Don't allow yourselves to be pulled down roads that lead to death, loss, and self-destruction. You are valuable, and someone else's treatment of you doesn't dictate your value.

Embrace your ability to say "no." You don't have to continue with a person who betrays your convictions, love, and standards. Remain calm and composed, and don't give into the sinful nature we can fall into when we are victims of betrayal. Remain holy as Christ is holy (Matthew 26:47-56). Remain faithful as He is faithful (Matthew 26:34).

The one who has betrayed or has been betrayed both need healing. They both need to release pain and accept forgiveness and comfort to move forward. We boldly live out our convictions so that we change the atmosphere around us and have those in darkness step into the light. You don't have to be your mistake or the mistake of others; we can choose to rise above it.

JEALOUSY

Where does your true power lie? Is it in your physical ability? Is it in how you treat others and how they treat you?

Your true power is in your ability to choose and make choices that align with your values and protect your peace. We are given the choice to decide how we will live our lives and how we want to impact the world. We can be the change we want to see in others. We can be an example of what we say is missing from the world, the church, in our families, and on our jobs.

It is not enough to know when things are off but also to have the boldness to live a life others can see as part of the Light. We are to bring hope wherever we go. Those in darkness will look at you, and some will marvel, and others may get jealous.

Jealousy is dangerous. It is unhealthy because we don't know what it takes for someone to achieve what they have. For all the good and not-so-good, we don't know what they did to arrive. We assume the road was bearable or even easy because they are here, and you can see them. You try to watch their movements, and their effortless actions make you think it is easy.

We underestimate time. We can sign ourselves up for other people's lives when we watch celebrities on television or on our phones. We can say we want their life, not knowing how well they sleep at night. We think the items we see in pictures or videos are real. Some things are posted, and it says underneath or in the comments this is an advertisement. My favorite sayings are results are not typical and objects are enlarged to show texture.

When we see these crafted props, we wonder why reality doesn't look like that. Why doesn't my whipped cream stick up or my milk mustache look appetizing? Because shaving cream is not tasty. What they use to create the looks that entice us is not real. Many of us get jealous and kill ourselves to have what others have when what they have is not real!

The smoking ads from years back made smoking look fun, cool, seductive, and sexy. They made many believe the hype that smoking will give you an edge. The only thing it gives is lung disease; it poisons you and those around you, and the high is fleeting, so you have to keep hitting it to not go into withdrawal. You are not free and happy, your face gets sunken in, you age like wildfire, and you can lose years of your life or your quality of life. Nothing is happy, sexy, or cool about that. Plus, it stank!

We can see the money of successful people and want their vacations, but we miss the rejection and emptiness that makes them necessary. The many nights they can spend alone in a large home or how they hide out in their office to avoid the disappointment their children have about them. The romantic relationships that are broken time and time again. We can miss our own pride and not see the lack of sincerity in others. We can be blinded and not recognize when something is jealousy or

JEALOUSY

honesty.

In a world where everyone feels entitled to share their thoughts regardless of their accomplishments or the lack thereof, we speak our minds. Not everyone, however, has the intent of being a solution. Some are here to distract you and deflect. They want you to loathe your happiness and fall into a pit that doesn't allow you to enjoy what you have. Their jealousy has made you the target because of their own unhappiness.

This is vanity, and they are chasing something they will never have because self-fulfillment is not outside in but inside out. Exodus 20:17 says, "You shall not covet your neighbor's house; you shall not covet your neighbor's wife, or his male servant, or his female servant, or his ox, or his donkey, or anything that is your neighbor's." This means you should not desire what belongs to someone else for yourself. We should not wish ourselves into someone else's marriage. To take someone else's beauty, things, money, etc.

To want these things directly implies what God has given you is not enough. Furthermore, it says He made a mistake with you and that you should have what someone else has. You should be someone else. Be in another body and have a different wife, husband, children, or life. It is a direct rejection of what you have to want to take someone else's life. This does not imply you are wrong for wanting more for yourself, but your desire to have what someone else has with a judging heart can lead to envy and not hope in Yah for the better.

If you love something more than you ought to, it can make you unsatisfied with everything you have. We serve a God who wants us to be grateful for what we already have. Yes, there is more. However, why would or should He give more if you still have food on your plate? Have you ever met people, specifically children, who are asking for seconds and have not finished what's already on their plate?

When we miss the blessing we already have, we can miss a step that connects us to what we are believing for. Instead of coveting or growing envious of others, we should look again at what we already have. Ecclesiastes 5:10 says, "He who loves money will not be satisfied with money, nor he who loves wealth with his income; this also is vanity."

Those who love anything out of proportion to Yah will never be satisfied. You can love money, looks, houses, wealth, cars, and other things more than God. If a person is in love with these things, that can make them chase their ambition unrighteously. Being motivated by envying what others have is not the way of Yah. He wants us to be cheerful givers, and it is hard to do that if we are jealous of what others are obtaining. It can be hard for us to be happy for someone else when we also need what they have, or we covet what they have.

This is a test and a lesson the Father gives to all of His children. The good news is there is no temptation that is new to man or a surprise to Him. Covetting what others have is an old trick and way of life He has already condemned. 1 Corinthians 10:13 reads, "No temptation has overtaken you that is not common to man. God is faithful, and He will not let you be tempted beyond your ability, but with the temptation, He will also provide the way of escape, that you may be able to endure it."

I know we can say stuff like, "I can't take this anymore." The enemy will try and talk us into believing we cannot endure seeing someone we wanted for ourselves happy. He will use our desire to have something we covet to inflict pain on ourselves. There are many psycho-thriller movies

JEALOUSY

where the character dresses up, cuts their hair, and does a character change to look like someone else they are hoping to replace. This is creepy and wrong and shows proof of an evil spirit taking hold of the situation.

When we are tempted to act out of jealousy to get what we want, God is bigger. The Word and the promises of Yah are stronger than envy and jealousy. The key to overcoming jealousy is to know that there is nothing that the Father cannot do. He will give each of us the measure we can endure.

Romans 12:3 says, "For by the grace given to me I say to everyone among you not to think of himself more highly than he ought to think, but to think with sober judgment, each according to the measure of faith that God has assigned." We each have a role to play in the Body of Christ and in life. If we feel rejected because of what others have, we need this scripture to release our joy.

We are all different, having unique gifts, traits, characters, and abilities. The Body of Christ is made up of many parts and not the same function, or we would not be a body but a single part working independently and not belonging to one another (Romans 7:4). No matter how small you feel or unimportant, every ligament, bone, organ, cell, and hair follicle plays an important role.

One gray hair can send a slew of thoughts to a person's mind. You would think one gray hair shouldn't change much; it is such a small change. Yet, day after day, people are worried about a single gray hair and the expected future of their hair going all white. Some instantly go out and buy die and don't have a second thought on whether the gray is what they like. Funny, you have twenty-year-olds with a head of gray hair by choice, and those growing into gray hair are running from it. Is it, not scripture fulfilled when it writes the eyes are never satisfied (Proverbs 27:20)?

When people are jealous, they seek to blame someone or take their pain out on others for why they don't have. When you see movies like "Wicked" and other people growing green with envy, they go through an experience of injustice or lack, and their emotions are shaped into hatred. They are living with a deep inset of disappointment and disinterest in being themselves, and they make an internal decision to leave their position for someone else's. A disassociated soul can grow angry and lean on jealousy for help. The hand they have been dealt, they cast it aside, thinking they cannot win with it. They wonder why I have to deal with this when others get that.

Jealous people who look at pretty women and desire to have what they have. They call pretty women ugly and talk about parts of their bodies they feel are not perfect. Not to be honest but to help them deal with their own self-loathing. They comment: "She has a pretty face but no booty" or "Cute feet, ugly teeth."

They have no shame in talking about trivial matters like hair or their sickness or disease. They have no regard for others because they have already chosen to disregard themselves. The imperfection they see within themselves, they search outwardly to find in others. They hold people to a mirror and have expectations that are warped by their pain.

The perfection they seek in themselves they project onto others and get angry when they don't care about them or exceed their expectations. It is sad how some people hope you fail so that they can gloat about your failure. Whether you succeed or fail bears no genuine change in their life, though. A person might laugh at your pain, but that doesn't

JEALOUSY

mean they feel something. People can laugh, tell jokes, and poke fun to hide their pain.

What they see in the mirror, they still see. For those who have been hurt by jealousy, I am sure you have heard that people act out because they don't have what you have. Because you are special and they are not in some way. You can sing, but they can't. For the person frequently hearing this, it can make you want to get rid of whatever makes you unique, especially if it is a trait like height, beauty, strength, power, or kindness. You can see your success as a curse because it brings others into harsh judgment and ends with you being isolated.

Growing up, I started to loathe being pretty. I know it sounds really silly. Who could hate being pretty? But I did. I hated being called pretty because it wasn't a topic of great happiness in my life. I have horror stories, and so does my mom for simply having hazel eyes, for being our complexion, growing up in hostile environments.

I remember one time my mom told me how she was chased home by six girls who didn't like her. These girls were bigger than her. They all had a boyfriend and some popularity at the school. My mom was a newcomer coming from an all-girls school. She had recently moved, and she wanted to fit in.

Only she didn't. Her hazel eyes and her having a mother, who looked white with Pocahontas' hair, made her a target. Girls couldn't call her names like "nappy head" or "pickaninny." She had beautiful hair. She wasn't fat but skinny. She didn't have boobs hardly, but she was proportioned and dressed well.

She wasn't a mean girl talking about everyone but minded her own business. She didn't chase boys, but they all loved her eyes and what she looked like. She never had to work to get admirers. She was a sweet person, pretty and smart, and she was a threat to the other girls who didn't look like her.

We would think colorism should be done with now, but unfortunately, it is still alive and well in many of our hearts. Those of a darker complexion may still question if they are as beautiful as women of a lighter complexion. A book that shows the unraveling some women feel is "To Kill A Brown Brown Girl." Some girls are being used because of what they are willing to do for a relationship or friends, and others are simply being themselves to gain popularity.

It can make you bitter when you have made compromising choices and others have done none of those things and can win the heart or interest of someone you favor. We can get desperate to have what we want and resort to the power of jealousy and envy to force our will. We can build a fantasy in our hearts and minds that can make it dangerous for others to know us. People who love something more than they should, if the hooks of jealousy grab them, could know no bounds to stop themselves from falling.

Those girls chased my mom that day for over four blocks. She ran screaming, and her grandmother heard her, as well as the rest of the

JEALOUSY

neighborhood, as the patty wagon of girls headed in the direction of her house. The girls didn't stop charging after her as the onlookers stepped outside their homes. They all kept going like an angry mob chasing her down the streets of Chicago. She felt relief when she saw her granddaddy emerge from the front door with a shotgun in hand.

"THE MONSTER"
K. LEE

The girls, blinded by rage and envy, quickly halted in place and swiftly turned around to head in the other direction. She learned that day that being pretty was no fault of her own but brought trouble along with compliments. She learned to fight because she had no choice. I know you have heard that saying, "You are too pretty to be out here fighting." Some don't know the stories of why many girls end up fighters.

It is written Job 5:2: "Surely vexation kills the fool, and jealousy slays the simple." We can be blinded by our rage to do something stupid like jump a girl because of what she looks like or has. We can get mad that the guy we liked didn't choose us and want to fight the girl they picked. Children aren't the only ones guilty of making stupid decisions out of jealousy or envy. Too many women are willing to kill and fight because of their emotions and belief in what is fair or theirs.

On the job, it can look different. It can be a new hire who came from a good school or a different location as a transfer. It can be someone with little experience with the company or less seniority. A family member who just came of age or someone who is affiliated with someone in the company who came highly recommended beats you out of a promotion.

It can feel unfair to realize your hard work is being overlooked and that someone who doesn't deserve it based on the time and circumstance required gets what you should have. The rules are put in place to help guard fairness, but when they are overlooked, they can make you go green with envy. You can question why the rules should bend for them. Who do they think they are? The longer you look, the more you see their imperfections, which makes you even angrier.

We will all make mistakes, but any mistake you see them make, you find yourself being hyper-critical of. You can use that mistake or action to defend your position on why they don't deserve what they have, and you do. We all look at people and how they live their lives to help us determine what we want out of life. It doesn't have to be on the strength of jealousy; it could serve as an example. But what happens when you can never achieve what someone else has? What happens if you have dark skin and you see a light-skinned woman living your dream?

What happens if the job or career you want requires education you don't have any time to squeeze in? Feeling antiquated and outdated because you are not familiar with computers and technology has many shrink back from the job force and leave it to the young people. That person could feel slighted and left with no resources to accomplish their goals.

The example they set their eyes on has

JEALOUSY

shown them the challenge and insurmountable odds facing them. It stops bringing positive encouragement and functions as a reservoir holding back what you had hoped to become. Looking at others can backfire if we feel inadequate from it instead of being encouraged.

What can we do to offset jealousy? How can we tame the feelings we have that are searching for an avenue to be expressed? How can we suppress the voice within us that speaks you deserve better and should have more at the extent of any costs?

How do we silence the voices that are not ours, that whisper in our ears? They say, "Why should they have it all when you work hard and put up with everyone's mess? You show up first and leave last. Why does everyone seem to get promoted over you? Why should you keep going when everything around you says stop!"

This voice wants nothing more than for you to give up on humanity. For you to stop being ethical, hopeful, and positive toward the future. It wants you to seek your own justice and make people do right by you. It creates a demand on yourself that you cannot bear, and it forces you to compete with a condition that isn't clearly defined or possible to recreate. It hopes you will get lost in your thoughts and emotions and lose sight of the true prize: You becoming and achieving what you were put on earth to complete. Jealousy is a distraction.

I love what Romans 12:12 says. It says, "Rejoice in hope, be patient in tribulation, be constant in prayer." Is hope good enough for you? Do you demand to see what you hope for and not have to tarry or wait for what you believe will come? If faith is the currency of heaven, how do we think we can pay in a different currency and that will be accepted or please Him so we can get what we want?

RELEASE PAIN

Faith, which is to hope for things and believe for them until they come, to act as if they are already here, though you work toward the manifestation of what was hoped for. It can seem like a conundrum to act as if something is done when it is not yet manifested in our reality. We may not be satisfied with how the supernatural world works.

The spiritual realm is not limited to what you can do with your hands or even see for yourself. It is based on what you can believe for, like a child full of imagination. Some things we desire will hit during our great, great, great children's generations, and we may not live to see them, but they will surely come. Can we be satisfied if we make a cake and others sit down to eat it?

Do you have to eat all of your food to appreciate what you have? Do we need to have the house we worked hard for to see the lessons of God? Can He show you an example of His faithfulness through someone else's life? Can He give someone else what you hoped to have, and you see that as a means to celebrate God? Seeing others happy and walking in their gift can be a moment that you, too, can rejoice. Seeing others make it is an example of how we, you, too, can make it.

I love watching documentaries and hearing biographies because I love to celebrate where people come from and the journey to making it. Many of them go from living in incredible circumstances to proving the power of God. Can you imagine growing up with no running water, toilets, plumbing, sufficient housing, heat, clothing, and the like in a mansion?

I love these stories for when people go from prison to the throne or when they were born poor and rise above their circumstances (Ecclesiastes 4:14). It is a difficult burden to fight the demon of

JEALOUSY

poverty and oppression. This is a stronghold over many people groups from all countries. We do not defeat this demon of jealousy without crushing the need to be self-seeking.

Proverbs 15:27 says, "Whoever is greedy for unjust gain troubles his own household, but he who hates bribes will live." The devil is good at offering bribes to get the Children of God to compromise. He offered Yashua all the riches on earth if He would bow down and worship him, and of course, He refused. Do you have the same answer when you are offered things on earth for compromise?

It can come easier, but it comes with a penalty. When we are discontent with what we have, we can easily lust for it and become envious of what others have. This action doesn't improve your life circumstances. It gives power to the enemy to use the pain you feel against you. Evil spirits love to twist your hopes into anxiety land mines to send you going in the wrong direction.

The Bible tells us, "Do not be anxious about anything, but in everything by prayer and supplication with thanksgiving let your requests be made known to God. 7 And the peace of God, which surpasses all understanding, will guard your hearts and your minds in Christ Jesus" (Philippians 4:7). Those plagued with envy and jealousy are not at peace in their hearts. Their separation from God and faith in Him has them chasing their own interest over the command of Yah to trust Him in all things.

There is value in each of our stories and encounters with the Father. Those with a grateful heart see Him more than those who complain or spend their time comparing oranges to apples. We are not the same people, no matter how many things may appear to look alike. What is your heart posture? Are you focused on your own self-ambition and not the heart of God?

James 3:16 says, "For where jealousy and selfish ambition exist, there will be disorder and every vile practice." When we are blinded by self-ambition, we can commit hideous acts against others. We can justify stealing, giving bribes, and accepting them. We can lose our purity and hope for the future. We are robbed of hope, and the hole is filled by the presence of evil spirits: jealousy, envy, and even self-sabotage.

Do you know that some evil spirits love to hang together to torment and conquer us? We are like sheep for the slaughter if we don't know the Word spoken about the battle going on within and around us (Romans 8:36). These spirits are together to bind us, to hold us, hostage in our hearts and minds by those who use spirits to manipulate and control. The villains allow their envy to push them to world domination and conquer not just their enemies but everyone in their close or distant proximity.

Jesus said, "But no one can enter a strong man's house and plunder his goods unless he first binds the strong man. Then indeed, he may plunder his house." How can the enemy make good by taking things from you if you are not first distracted by his antics?

Before we can lose a battle, we have to be convinced that there is no battle. We have to believe that someone or something can take what Yah said. We have to believe that their power is greater than the Father's ability to turn all things to our Good!

In Romans 8:28 it reads, "And we know that for those who love God, all things work together for good, for those who are called according to his

JEALOUSY

purpose." This verse and promise should stir your heart to believe–to hope. I know it is hard to see how someone stealing or taking something from you could be used by God.

If you have lost a job, career, car, your health, income, a spouse, or house, it is a blow to the gut. Nothing can prepare you for it when it happens, kind of like being dragged underwater. You can see it coming, but it still takes your breath away. So, how can the Father get glory out of our loss to those who envy us and plot our demise? But oh, I tell you, those who take unjustly will find out something about taking what belongs to others.

Proverbs 28:22 says, "A stingy man hastens after wealth and does not know that poverty will come upon him." The things they invest in and put their faith in will bring about poverty. Poverty is more than the lack of money, houses, and things. You can be poor in spirit, confidence, knowledge, health, or wealth.

What wealth have they stored in heaven for miracles? What wealth have they stored to solve an incurable disease by the power of I AM? What have they done to have peace in their hearts that surpasses all understanding? What glory rests on them that brings favor no matter the circumstance? What is holding up their castles when the walls shake, and their people turn on them?

I tell you, like Zephaniah has said in 1:18, "Neither their silver nor their gold shall be able to deliver them on the day of the wrath of the Lord. In the fire of His jealousy, all the earth shall be consumed; for a full and sudden end He will make of all the inhabitants of the earth." The way people treat you, the Father will judge. How you act, the Father will judge. Nothing gets past Him, but all are subject to His authority and sovereignty.

RELEASE PAIN

Don't be tempted to envy a man of violence and do not choose any of his ways (Proverbs 3:31). Those who think that bending the rules to their benefit will get them somewhere unlawfully will come to a crashing halt. All the wealth they accumulated will be returned or given away. They will return back to what they were before. So many who grow to fame lose it all. Those who amass a lot of wealth lose it all. Those who thought storing up what they desired would make life sweet find it means nothing if they cannot enjoy it.

Better is a little with the peace of Yah than to humble yourself to the plans of the enemy to obtain wealth and possessions (Proverbs 15:16). Have you ever read Ecclesiastes 4:4-8? I love it because it sums up the lives we will live if we are motivated by envying or coveting what others have. We will never be satisfied, and we will happily work our bodies to the ground for things that hold no joy. They are not the key to what we need; they don't point to a solution, and they have us toling–chasing something aimlessly that we can never find.

King Solomon writes, "Then I saw that all toil and all skill in work come from a man's envy of his neighbor. This also is vanity and a striving after wind. 5 The fool folds his hands and eats his own flesh. 6 Better is a handful of quietness than two hands full of toil and a striving after wind. 7 Again, I saw vanity under the sun: 8 one person who has no other, either son or brother, yet there is no end to all his toil, and his eyes are never satisfied with riches, so that he never asks, "For whom am I toiling and depriving myself of pleasure?" This also is vanity and an unhappy business."

Is this not how we sound when we work only to miss time with our children who don't know us as we get older? We look at the tree at Christmas time–if you do that kind of thing, and feel guilty

JEALOUSY

we don't have more. We don't spend enough time reflecting on the Messiah; we are worried about the gifts and training our children to do the same, but what about love?

Is that under the tree? In the house? In your heart–their hearts? Or are you the Black, Asian, White, Hip, Tanned Santa Clause they can't wait to drop off a gift they will forget about before next year as you hop back to work! Proud of a toy, necklace, vacuum, or other goods that your heart wasn't in, back to plowing, striving after the wind.

We focus on lack during a bountiful celebration period. The Messiah that takes away the sins of the world, we are worried about people's emotions for not having what they wanted and nothing about what they refuse to receive at Christmas. We are robbed of the Peace that the King provides because many are letting the enemy bind us in distractions.

The lack of love causes envy, strife, pain, and jealousy. When some see it on others and not on themselves, they can become bitter. Have you ever wondered how December is the month most people commit suicide, yet it is the month that we celebrate the birth of the Savior, the Prince of Peace? I found the stat confounding since we are to exemplify Him the most at this time than all year long. But could it be that seeing the love in your life, in your smile, in your hope causes a void so deep to those who don't have Him?

Yah is Love. 1 John 4:7-8 reads, "Beloved, let us love one another, for love is from God, and whoever loves has been born of God and knows God. 8 Anyone who does not love does not know God, because God is love." What would a person do when they are blinded by the pain of the absence of love? This loss, this missing link, can make many see no reason to live on. Where can they hide where

Yah is not there? The I AM that I AM is all and all (1 Corinthians 15:28), and if they reject and run from Him, where do they go?

     Jealousy and self-sabotage make a man furious, and he will not spare himself when he takes revenge (Proverbs 6:34). Suicide is a manifestation of self-sabotage. Unresolved pain from the lack of something or someone can push people to a point where they choose not to recover. We know the Hand of Yah can restore anything, rescuing many from the gates of hell and the grave (Revelation 1:18).

     Envy of others can lead to the death of who you were born to become. For those who are jealous of you, you may not see what they see or know that you have what they want. They can pick on you. Call you names and speak limiting thoughts and ideas over your future and life.

     We used to say, prayerfully not no more, he picks on you because he likes you. Now, we know he picks on you because he is envious of the one who will have you. When people don't feel they measure up, and they want to, they can take their jealousy out on you. Don't let them.

     They should rise to the occasion or watch you win with someone else–but please don't believe their lies. Don't listen to the voice that kills your love and hope. You are something. You are somebody. You are loved and called by Yah to be something.

     No matter where you come from or what it looks like now, have hope in His power to lift you up and restore what anyone has taken or darkened about you. Don't give away to others what belongs to you. Don't believe you have nothing because you don't have money or things. Don't believe you are

JEALOUSY

only something because of those around you. Your value is not generated because you are married or divorced.

I know it is easy to speak hope when you can see the light at the end of the tunnel. I remember when I had to leave Florida for Georgia in hopes of a better life and future. I had less than $5,000 and had to start over. I had no job, no house, no apartment, and a blank space in my renting history. I was nervous, and I thought I didn't have what it took to make it. I was scared, and before I got to a point where I would envy my soon-to-be ex-husband, the Father would catch me.

He reminded me of my heart and mindset when I was married. I spent many nights avoiding the empty spaces in my 5 bedroom home. I picked the house, and it was gorgeous. It had a pool, tiled floors, two sitting areas, a man cave, and a large office for me with a bathroom. The second floor had a sitting area with a patio and it came partially furnished.

We got new furniture, and as I looked around, I envied those who could have all this with the peace and love of Yah. Who could be married with a baby and see and feel the love of Yah? I didn't have that love from my husband, but I learned to accept what he could give me at the time. I ignored the signs of misdealings and just kept living with my head in the clouds.

When I left my corporate job to take care of our child, he didn't approve. He told me he would not help me with my choice, and he didn't make it easy on me. He envied me being home while he worked outside the home. He once told me that he might want to stay home while I go out to work. I never experienced a relationship where I did not work just as much as my husband and even paid more, if not all, of my bills as if I were single.

I shut down inside, and I began to pour thoughts into my heart to make me believe this was the life I was meant to live. I took God and the hope of a healthy, loving marriage out of the equation. I saw what I could see, and I believed for so little. When the marriage ended, like the Hebrews, I wanted to go back to Egypt even if my heart and hope were in chains.

Life is not always roses, and when we see the life we hope to live being experienced by others, it can bring a cloud over our heads that is not so easy to shake. When I had to pawn my wedding ring while he lived off the money he made while married to me, it hurt. While I worked two jobs that were flexible with our daughter's daycare schedule and my desire to be the biggest influence on her life, I had little support from him to watch her with me.

He saw the value in going out to work and wanted me to do the same, but I didn't agree. I enjoy being around my children, and I started praying for that. I unconsciously put Yah in a box and thought getting a job meant being away from home more than I was around. I saw the limited life and not the abundant life. I kept praying all the while I worked to get to the house I longed to own.

My credit score wasn't past 634, but I expected to be a homeowner. Not because I envied others but because I dared to believe and put my hope in God again to achieve what I could not. I saw the facts concerning my life, but I dared to believe Him over my facts! I remember walking around the outside of the house I picked with no bank that would give me a house loan. I had a job for less than 3 months, and my savings were still low.

JEALOUSY

I had way more going in the no category than the yes, but God! I got the house through an arrangement with the owner. All the repairs were afforded through a credit line one bank would give me. I was able to build a home for my daughter. I learned a valuable lesson in obtaining this house. When we are willing to serve and align our belief with His power and best, we open the door for Him to demonstrate a glimpse of what our best could look like here on earth.

EMPOWERING SCRIPTURES: INJUSTICE

Revelation 1:18 and the living one. I died, and behold, I am alive forevermore, and I have the keys of Death and Hades.

1 John 4:7-8 Beloved, let us love one another, for love is from God, and whoever loves has been born of God and knows God. 8 Anyone who does not love does not know God, because God is love.

1 Corinthians 15:28 When all things are subjected to him, then the Son himself will also be subjected to him who put all things in subjection under him, that God may be all in all.

Proverbs 15:16 Better is a little with the fear of the Lord than great treasure and trouble with it.

Romans 8:28 And we know that for those who love God, all things work together for good, for those who are called according to his purpose.

Mark 3:27 But no one can enter a strong man's house and plunder his goods unless he first binds the strong man. Then, indeed, he may plunder his house.

Romans 8:36 As it is written, "For your sake, we are being killed all the day long; we are regarded as sheep to be slaughtered."

Romans 7:4 Likewise, my brothers, you also have died to the law through the body of Christ, so that you may belong to another, to him who has been raised from the dead, in order that we may bear fruit for God.

Romans 12:3 For by the grace given to me I say to everyone among you not to think of himself more highly than he ought to think, but to think with sober judgment, each according to the measure of faith that God has assigned.

Ecclesiastes 5:10 He who loves money will not be satisfied with money, nor he who loves wealth with his income; this also is vanity.

Proverbs 27:20 Sheol and Abaddon are never satisfied, and never satisfied are the eyes of man.

Philippians 4:6-7 Do not be anxious about anything, but in everything by prayer and supplication with thanksgiving let your requests be made known to God. 7 And the peace of God, which surpasses all understanding, will guard your hearts

JEALOUSY

and your minds in Christ Jesus.

Proverbs 15:27 Whoever is greedy for unjust gain troubles his own household, but he who hates bribes will live.

James 3:16 For where jealousy and selfish ambition exist, there will be disorder and every vile practice.

1 John 5:4 For everyone who has been born of God overcomes the world. And this is the victory that has overcome the world—our faith.

Galatians 5:19-21 Now the works of the flesh are evident: sexual immorality, impurity, sensuality, 20 idolatry, sorcery, enmity, strife, jealousy, fits of anger, rivalries, dissensions, divisions, 21 envy, drunkenness, orgies, and things like these. I warn you, as I warned you before, that those who do such things will not inherit the kingdom of God.

Ecclesiastes 4:4-8 Then I saw that all toil and all skill in work come from a man's envy of his neighbor. This also is vanity[a] and a striving after wind. 5 The fool folds his hands and eats his own flesh. 6 Better is a handful of quietness than two hands full of toil and a striving after wind. 7 Again, I saw vanity under the sun: 8 one person who has no other, either son or brother, yet there is no end to all his toil, and his eyes are never satisfied with riches, so that he never asks, "For whom am I toiling and depriving myself of pleasure?" This also is vanity and an unhappy business.

Proverbs 6:34 For jealousy makes a man furious, and he will not spare when he takes revenge.

Zephaniah 1:18 Neither their silver nor their gold shall be able to deliver them on the day of the wrath of the Lord. In the fire of his jealousy, all the earth shall be consumed, for a full and sudden end he will make of all the inhabitants of the earth.

Proverbs 28:22 A stingy man hastens after wealth and does not know that poverty will come upon him.

1 Corinthians 10:13 No temptation has overtaken you that is not common to man. God is faithful, and he will not let you be tempted beyond your ability, but with the temptation, he will also provide a way of escape so that you may be able to endure it.

Romans 12:12 Rejoice in hope, be patient in tribulation, be constant in prayer.

Exodus 20:17 You shall not covet your neighbor's house; you shall not covet your neighbor's wife, or his male servant, or his female servant, or his ox, or his donkey, or anything that is your neighbor's.

Ecclesiastes 4:14 For he went from prison to the throne, though in his own kingdom, he had been born poor.

1 Corinthians 13:4 Love is patient and kind; love does not envy or boast; it is not arrogant

Job 5:2 Surely vexation kills the fool, and jealousy slays the simple.

Proverbs 3:31 Do not envy a man of violence and do not choose any of his ways

Romans 10:11 For the Scripture says, "Everyone who believes in him will not be put to shame."

Proverbs 6:27 Can a man carry fire next to his chest and his clothes not be burned?

JEALOUSY

1 Peter 1:13 Therefore, preparing your minds for action and being sober-minded, set your hope fully on the grace that will be brought to you at the revelation of Jesus Christ.

Hebrews 13:5 Keep your life free from the love of money, and be content with what you have, for he has said, "I will never leave you nor forsake you."

Song of Song 8:6 Set me as a seal upon your heart, as a seal upon your arm, for love is strong as death, jealousy[a] is fierce as the grave. Its flashes are flashes of fire, the very flame of the Lord.

YOUR POWER AND FOUNDATION

To curb the urge of jealousy, envy, or self-sabotage, we must believe that God has an expected end for our lives. That your being here has a purpose and you are not forgotten. I love that song by Israel Holton, "I Am Not Forgotten, God Knows My Name." The lyrics are so true, and we need them when we feel low or think of speaking against His plans for our lives.

RELEASE PAIN

We cannot help that others want to be us, but people wanting to be like you isn't all bad, either. We need to focus on how we can become great and not get bogged down by others' opinions. God is a jealous God, and He shares His glory with no one (Deuteronomy 4:24). "The Lord your God is a consuming fire, a jealous God."

Nothing can stand in the presence of Yah so as to take His priority over your life, and there be no fallout. To keep Him in His proper place in your life, you will have to prepare your mind to be affixed on His goodness and not your circumstances. Some of us have been judged and singled out because of our greatest attributes.

When we are tormented for doing right, it doesn't make us feel good. It can make us angry, bitter, or lackluster toward believing and hoping for something better. We can feel like we are in sinking sand, and it is hard to get out of the mud, cementing us to limitations. How do you get unstuck and stay above the liquid line? You have to set your gaze on someone who is holding out a pole to save you.

UNSTUCK
DR. SHANNON SIMPSON SANDS

We have to reach our hands out and accept the pole extended to us to take action on what we hope for and release the weight on our legs. If you feel like you are tired of fighting and being the single woman or man out, don't give up now. Take action and keep your thoughts hopeful that His grace is sufficient to bring you a Word that will save

JEALOUSY

you in the place you are in.

1 Peter 1:13 says, "Therefore, preparing your minds for action, and being sober-minded, set your hope fully on the grace that will be brought to you at the revelation of Jesus Christ (the Word)."

So, what is the revelation of the Word? What did the Father submit to us through His Son that can save us from jealousy, envy, and coveting our neighbors' things and lifestyles? To keep yourself from jealousy, you want to keep free from the love of money and be content with what you have (Hebrews 3:5). Why? Because Hebrews 13:5 goes on to say, "I will never leave you nor forsake you." When you know you are not alone, there is nothing He won't do to save you out of quicksand.

There is a Word for you, and when we desire or love something more than God, we can sacrifice things and lead ourselves to quicksand. We can ignore the Word and focus on our own desires, wants, and ambitions. We can be so absorbed in what we want for our lives that we miss what Yah is asking of our lives at that moment. Don't miss this.

Yah is strong enough to use any circumstance to bless His children. He can use what we do to ourselves and what others commit against us to lead us in the right direction. Set the Father as a seal upon your heart, as a seal upon your arm, for love is strong as death, jealousy is fierce as the grave. Its flashes are flashes of fire, the very flame of the Lord (Song of Song 8:6). Seal your desires in the ears of Yah. Trust Him to hear your heart and know the plans He has for you. When you love, you will weigh down the weight of unrighteous jealousy.

Jealousy is an emotion reserved for Yah because it is too much power for us as humans to yield it and not sin. Can we take fire into our bosom, our hands, our hearts, and not be burned (Proverbs 6:27)? Yah is a consuming fire, so fire with fire will cause no pain. He can extinguish the fire or fires in your life–and He does that for those who love Him and are called according to His purpose (Romans 8:28). Trust Him and see that you will not be put to shame no matter what it looks like (Romans 10:11).

JEALOUSY

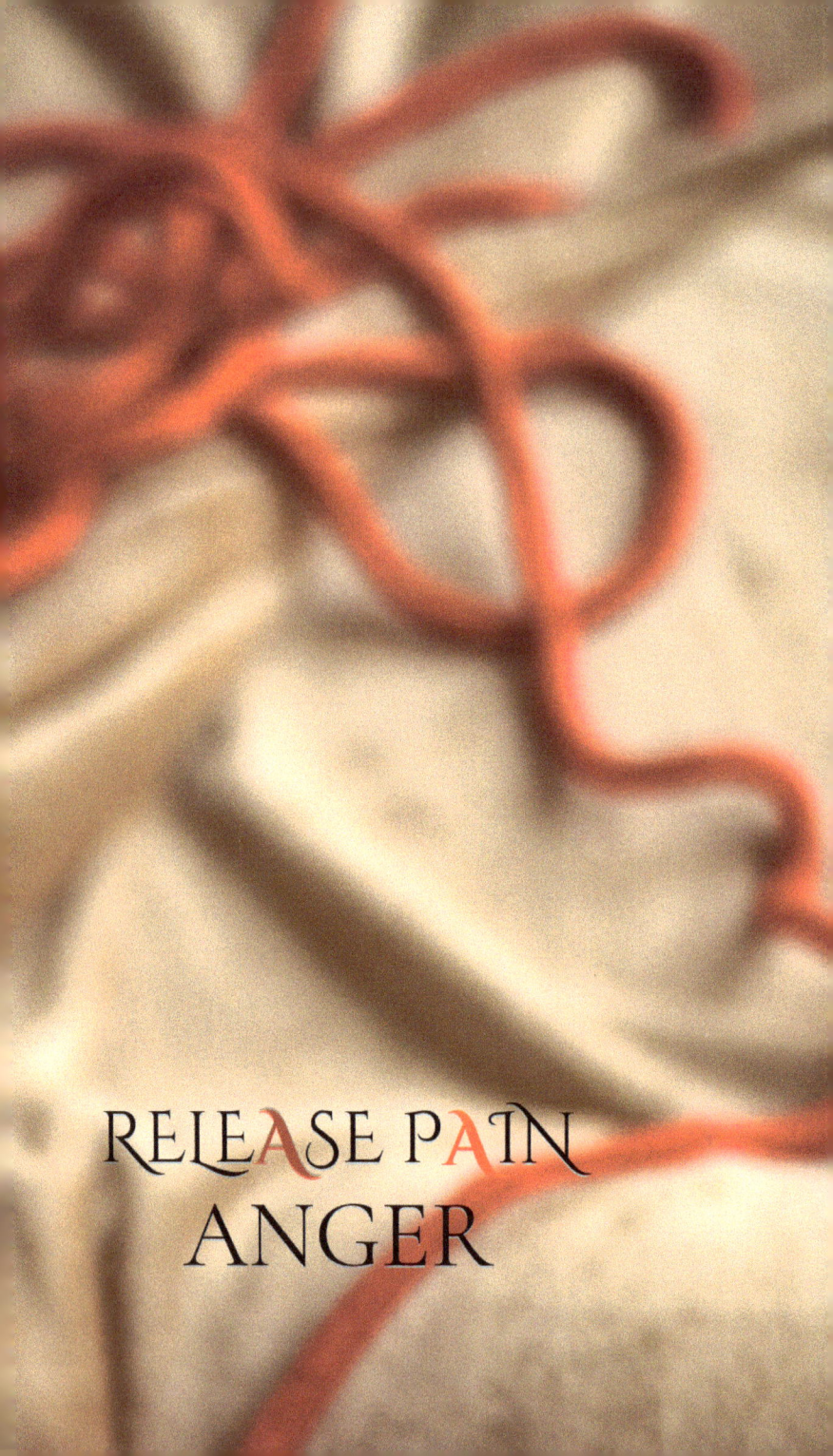

ANGER

The greatest threat that taps the shoulders of every man, woman, boy, and girl is anger. This is the easiest emotion and perhaps the quickest one we learn, even as a child. A baby can get angry and start screaming when he or she does not get what they want. Anger doesn't have to be righteous or even understandable. It can be selfish, ruthless, and even heartless.

We can sit by the baby, rock the baby, sing to the baby, and even try to change diapers and please them by making silly faces. Some children are so angry that nothing will break their desire to cry. Yes, sometimes pain can be the reason we cry and demand the attention of others, but often, we are angry and that power is fueling our actions.

Do you struggle with anger? I have to admit, in my life, I have had some strong battles with anger. I could be trying to focus, and the noise that I could easily blank out normally when deadlines are pressing seems to push me over the edge. It seems to make me bubble over like boiling water in a pot on the stove, and I can speak through tight lips, "No."

I am not yelling, but I am also not using my normal tone. We can all be triggered by someone or something and not act like our normal selves. It can be disappointing to work hard at something, and the results are far less than expected. It can make your heart heavy and render you powerless. Out of that strong emotion, it can give access for anger to take hold of you.

I don't like it when I cannot control the pressure happening within me, and my emotions are overrun by the spirit of anger. Any of us can get angry, and it is a natural reaction that we all utilize. But did you know that the Bible records it is not good that any man should be angry? James 1:19-20 says, "Know this, my beloved brothers: let every person be quick to hear, slow to speak, slow to anger; 20 for the anger of man does not produce the righteousness of God."

I have had to talk to myself to keep calm when I have been disappointed. If I am frustrated or getting pushed to my max with patience. I know the exercise to count to ten, something we have all heard by now. When we get angry, it doesn't produce positive endorphins, and we know when it starts to pump in our blood. We feel the anger and the dark side it brings out of us. It can scare us as we become more sensitive to our emotions.

I try to keep myself balanced, not so that I wouldn't fight somebody, but so that I could keep my spirit up. I love being in the light and sensing the darkness that comes from anger I don't like it. It is so easy to fall into the spirit of offense when we are angry too and say or do things we wouldn't do with a level head.

Some would think that getting angry when we are disrespected should be expected. The need to defend yourself seems too welcomed when someone oversteps your boundaries, too. We can forget about Proverbs 19:11, which reads, "Good

ANGER

sense makes one slow to anger, and it is his glory to overlook an offense." We don't care at that moment about who gets the glory from our actions, but when we respond out of our unrighteous anger, we will give glory to the enemy with our actions.

Yah looks on the heart and knows us (1 Samuel 16:7). How do you handle being angry? Do you throw things? Yell at people? Talk negatively about yourself or others. Are you giving glory to God with your response or showering gifts upon the kingdom of darkness? There is a healthy way to process anger and many ways to improperly do so. However, if you want to skate away from anger, you have to be willing to drop offenses quickly.

One of the guilty pleasures we all have is verbally fighting with the cars around us. Don't we all have a spirit of outrage, even road rage, that can creep up on us and have us yelling at people who can't hear us? Some of us throw up our hands when we speak and tell whoever will listen about how dumb they are acting and why they shouldn't have a license. Then, should they hear us, we can feel embarrassed about how we were acting, especially if they are apologetic or bigger and stronger.

I saw a man park his car on the street and yell at another driver who didn't seem as confident in his jacked-up truck as before. My sister was sideswiped and ran off the road by a truck like this. She chased the truck and got his details, but the cop said because she pursued him, she couldn't file a complaint. Seems very wrong to me. How else was she supposed to get his plate if he sped off afterward?

Is it me, or have you noticed that when we are angry, there is a surge of power pumping through our bodies that makes us feel as if we could run a marathon? The Incredible Hulk didn't have as much power when he wasn't big and green–he was smart but not scary and powerful. Do we feel that way too? When we are mild and agreeable, everyone takes us for a joke. But when we get angry, real mad, all of a sudden, people start to back up and respect our position. They could even say, "That woman is crazy. You need to leave her alone." or "Don't mess with that dude. I don't think his head is screwed on tight."

But why does it have to come to us getting out of character for people to regard our opinions and respect our boundaries? This intentional form of ignorance is enough to make most of us want to slap someone out of rage. How could someone be so insensitive when I can feel all of these emotions from their rejections? We think they cannot be human or that they have no heart.

When someone calls you a racial slur, for many of us, our initial response isn't to laugh it off. Our eyebrows raise up, and our head gently shakes from left to right. We were dazed for a quick second, as if someone slapped us in the face real quick. We are so shocked that many of us have them repeat it. It is when they repeat it that something usually happens.

When we are angry, we have this uncontrollable power almost to throw things, push people, and say reckless words. We can respond before we think or have time to consider the repercussions of our actions. Those who lead the best marches and plan non-violent ways to handle conflict must prepare people to be insulted and not respond. How can you hear someone curse you out or spit on you and not respond?

I don't know how people sat at restaurants to protest their rights to be there. I am sure glad we can live off the backs of their bravery and calm. Being angry takes up more energy and commitment than being calm. However, it takes more strength to be calm during a challenging time. It is easy to suppress hurts, pains, and afflictions from being at the top of your mind when there are other worthy causes fighting for its attention.

We are to forgive others for their offenses against us so we can free up the mental real estate and the heart space and put something else there. So many of us cannot enjoy what is in front of us because we are still angry about what just happened. When we leave an incident or a situation arises, we can stew over the actions of others for hours, days, months, or even years.

Some things arguably will take time to heal from, and feeling powerless to change an incident can make us rehash the experience and see if there is something else we could do. For those who have been assaulted, we can get angry that it ever happened. We can be mad at the people involved and even more pissed off with the people who didn't help. I heard a news article where a group of children went to boil hot water at a slumber party. There was a child who was sleeping, and out of the blue, this group of kids thought it would be funny to throw boiling hot water on the boy.

The skin on his face melted off like butter, and of course, his parents were angry. They went to the extent of pressing charges on all of the children who were present and any adult who could be found negligent in the matter. The children who were responsible for boiling the water and throwing it on the boy said they were pranking him. But this proposed prank cost this child his face. It could have killed his self-confidence and made him live his life in the shadows. How could this ever be funny?

RELEASE PAIN

For some of us, people have done things to us that have robbed us of feeling our sense of self. We have been violated in a grave way. When we should have been safe, we were put in a dangerous position due to no mistake on our part. How could a person not be filled with wrath, anger, or hatred if someone intentionally caused us pain for laughs or their own self-fulfillment? No one wants to be a victim of hazing or abuse to fit in. It is wrong to abuse anyone in any way and to have enjoyment in someone else's pain. It makes a person question, what has gotten a hold of me to where pain makes me feel love?

Love is kind, patient, long-suffering, and it endures troubles (1 Corinthians 13:4-7). It doesn't seek to bully, dominate, control, manipulate, and inflict pain for self-promotion or gratification. None of this is of God, of Love. We should not take enjoyment in other people's pain, but we can appreciate justice being served. There are times when justice supersedes what others consider mercy. Those children wanted mercy and not to be tried for attempted murder. However, if they were tried or not, in both cases, it could be said they had mercy. None of them had done to them what they did to someone else.

An eye for an eye, and a tooth for a tooth, is in the Bible (Matthew 5:38). This verse deals with cause and effect. If you do this to someone, this is the penalty of such an action. What you do to others will be done unto you. How you treat people will also be how people treat you. Even how you judge people, you too will be judged (Matthew 7:1-2).

So, what does this say about retaliation? This is not talking about self-defense but the spirit of offense. How do you overcome the spirit of offense? But not responding in the same way it treat-

ANGER

ed you? If it slapped you in the face with a negative comment, don't allow that comment to bury within you or have you retaliate with another cutting word. We are to bring peace and love.

The enemy would like nothing more than for you both to leave a conversation, argument, or situation, being the loser. If two married people don't learn how to love each other instead of retaliating during conversations, how can love overcome all? We have to suffer injustice so that justice can come. Christ, the Messiah, had to suffer for our sins so that we could be redeemed. If we suffer nothing, how then can we share in His blessings and suffering (1 Peter 4:13)?

If we are redeeming ourselves, what need would we have for a redeemer (Galatians 3:13)? He took on sin, bearing our sins at the cross, even becoming sin, so that we can be reconciled to Yah. He made a way for us to get back to the Father when we were still sinners, undeserving, backbiters, revelers, adulterers, fornicators, liars, thieves, and the rest. But His mercy, that He requires we show, some people have determined not to be the example of His Word personified. They have decided that His suffering needs to continue alone without their support.

If we are righting wrongs against us, what need would we have for vengeance to be the Lord's (Romans 12:19)? The Father tells us through Paul not to avenge ourselves. Why? Because He told us to be blameless. We are to be holy because He is holy. He is just, and vengeance He has said belongs to Him. Will a man rob God? We rob Him of His glory if we avenge ourselves by getting even and scooping down low when He says come higher, son or daughter.

If we ditch out what was ditched to us, what

glory have we stored up in heaven (Matthew 5:46)? It is not counted to us as righteousness if someone makes fun of our hair and we talk about their clothes. If they point out our faults and we point to theirs, where can healing take place? We have to be on topic, and arguing other points when another matter is brought up does not bring resolution.

When we can learn to cover each other's sins, that is how we win a brother or sister over to the power of the Word. The Word is to be used as a weapon against the power of principalities, systems, and evil rulers. Not for it to be used amongst people who need healing. We are not to weaponize the Word to kill and destroy people but the powers of the enemy working through people.

What coals have we poured over the blaze to simmer it down, but to the contrary, we have put fuel to the fire, and it burns more through retaliation (Romans 12:20). Do you want to defuse anger or grow the blaze within your heart? Do you want your pain or the pain of others to push your buttons continually? None of us can handle the power of anger unfiltered by the Word.

Likewise, none of us can afford to reap what we have sown. We have all fallen short of the glory of the Most High (Romans 3:23). So, on what righteous standing can we argue why others had to suffer our pain, but we must suffer no pain? We, too, will suffer because it is part of the life of being a believer. Will you disown God now that you know suffering is also tied to blessings?

When we sit and rehash other people's faults and report them to Yahshua, like Martha, He knows we have further to grow. How much effort and power have we put into things not worthy of our attention or time? She was complaining to the Messiah about how she had no help and that Mary

ANGER

wasn't doing her part. Some of us want to call on God to retaliate for us. But they don't know the spirit of God who searches the hearts of man. He knows who He will choose to have mercy on and those who see that laying at His feet is better than being busy performing useless actions.

When we stop talking in an argument, have you noticed that some people get angry? They get frustrated to the point that in violent relationships, they hit you for not speaking. When you are uncertain and speak low, they get mad, but you fuel their narcissistic desire to be smart so they aren't angry. But it is when you sound wise they boil over. The Bible says that fools will sound wise if they stop talking (Proverbs 17:28).

When you don't know what to say, it is best to keep quiet. The longer you keep your peace and your calm and let them speak, the clearer your direction and communication become. It is unwise to cast your pearls before swine (Matthew 7:6). Not everyone will appreciate the intelligence you bring, and it might be best to keep silent instead of yelling.

I was in a relationship, and he would make accusations against me to hide his insecurities. He would say I was going to leave him for a younger man and that I would leave him for someone with more money. I was looking at my options, and that's why I didn't want to marry him, etc. At first, I got angry. I yelled back to defend myself when he yelled or accused me of stuff I wasn't doing. But I was convicted afterward, and I realized this was not how I would win this battle.

I tried a different path and chose to keep quiet instead. I saw him squirm like a worm on a hook, and it wasn't my hook he was on. He was offended, in pain, and had a deep-seated insecurity that would flare its head when he felt I was thinking too much for myself. It bothered him when I didn't agree with his logic. He claimed his way was not only right but the only way to feel about the situation because he had all this training and years of experience.

He even told me once in an argument that he was my senior and that I was being disrespectful in disagreeing with him. I did not speak but allowed him to talk for two hours about protocol and how I was to behave when talking to him. After he was done, I did not point out his flaws. I did see how what he said violated several scriptures we both knew. I simply replied, "Thanks for sharing your opinions on this matter. I will pray about this."

He disagreed that what he had said was an opinion, and I replied, "I can understand how you feel that way. I do thank you for being transparent and making sure there is no ambiguity about how you feel." I knew better than to share how I felt, especially if it went against what he just said. Some things are a difference in opinion amongst people, and others, a difference in theology. Our differences were small, but our difference in spirit was large.

I was not the type of person, nor am I today, to hold on to things in the past. I let it go. I choose not to be a vessel to hold the accounts of other people's flaws. I also don't want to be a vessel holding on to pain. I try my best to let go of anything that I know will distract me from doing what I should do. Sometimes, to let it go, I write a journal entry in a book because writing is my therapy. I can clean the house because clutter makes my brain discombobulated. I don't want any of my thoughts or pain to morph into worrying.

We are to cast our burdens on Yah, but it is hard to do that when we are intentional about solving our own problems. He wanted us to solve

ANGER

problems that were beyond the both of us. Have you ever tried to have a relationship with someone who wanted you to pay for other people's decisions or their pain? When someone has secretly made up in their heart to go over your faults and keep score, it is not a relationship of love but judgment. Holding on to the mistakes of other people to the point where you penalize others will cost you more pain.

I remember a guy who was dating a woman. The two of them were older. He had been married many times, and the woman had been married many times, too. Whenever the two of them got into a disagreement, he would bring up his exes and say that they were cheaters and cruel to him. He projected his anger towards the woman he was dating and would say mean things that I even heard a time or two. I did mention it and said, "I don't think you should talk to anyone like that. We can all make mistakes, but this woman is not stupid."

He would automatically assume argumentative answers in their conversations. When we are hurting, leaking, and angry at the way things have gone, we can unintentionally take it out on others. Simple issues we can blow out of proportion and treat like an atomic bomb fell in the living room when it was an innocent oversight. The two of them could go from having a good time drinking and talking to fighting with their words about the other's faults.

He would say that women are no good, and they are all the same, as he flicked his hands to dismiss any other conclusion. She would get angry at his gesture and reply, "Women aren't all bad. You are just angry. You need to forgive them and yourself. These relationships are from decades ago."

He would reply to her comment in rage, "You don't know the pain they caused me. You don't know what they did to me. How can you tell me how to get over it? I paid the child support to her, and she is still sending lawyers after me. I am fifty years old now, and I don't work. How am I supposed to have a life and pay her too?"

He was angry. The woman was right. But she did not know how to help him release the pain he felt. He didn't know what he needed to do to get free. What ultimately broke up the dysfunctional couple was rage. The woman also had skeletons in her past, that she also didn't get past. She had a mother who didn't protect her. Her mother would leave for days to chase men she wanted to marry.

Some of the guys she married turned out to be molesters, abusers, and thieves. She married a man who violated her daughters, beat her up, and took her money! She wanted to be loved, and she didn't get the love she was looking for from her children and family. She wanted a man's love. There is nothing wrong with that, but when the love you crave is damaging, toxic, abusive, and painful, there is a lot wrong with it.

That woman grew to drink and find her own means of coping. When the two of them would argue, she poked to his pain with ex-wives, and he poked at her childhood that makes her drink nightly. They both had pain, and they both had anger. They both were running and handling their anger somewhat differently, but neither was the victor.

On an eventful night, she was drinking, and he had a stroke. The arguing and the stress affected his health. The warnings his daughter gave him about relaxing and not allowing anyone to get him that angry were ignored. The daughter told her mother and father they were not a good match if they could not find a way to heal together. They were not focused on healing but doing the same

ANGER

old same. They both stayed in their own ways and leaned on their past to draw their future.

After he returned home after his second stroke, he had two in a short period; he was tired and restless from having COVID-19 while trying to rehabilitate after losing the mobility of his right side. It was a scary time and a time when he may not remember all that he had done. On this particular night, while he was trying to rest, the woman tried to speak to him while she had a can of beer in her hands. His frustration with her inability to stay sober gave him the power to yoke her up against a wall and put her in a fight or flight mode.

The bond that they had, which was doomed from the start under the circumstances, was broken. They broke up, and neither is the victor. In so many conversations, you would have thought one of them could have stopped long enough to assess the situation. One of them would sense the danger, like how we feel when running up on a snake, bear, or wolf, and adjust their posture to start backing up and looking for an exit slowly.

I wished there had been something to distract or lower the energy in the room between the two of them on too many occasions. But sometimes, the inevitable happens, and you have to outrun a snake, wolf, or bear. Anger can make you overlook what is right in front of you. You can see people using violence as a way of projecting control when they sense you slipping from their grips.

Some are mentally abusive as he was, but the physical abuse, although not fully intentional, still happened. Not everyone's abusive situation is accidental. Some spouses can see their wives dressing up to go out or are in a good mood, which disrupts their spirit. It makes you wonder what kind of spirit is this, right? An abusive person can do something or say something that attempts to have that woman second-guess her plans or question if she should be happy if he is not.

She can regress to a room and cry instead of staying in that light atmosphere that brings comfort. Now, she is enclosed in a cage to be under a microscope, and she has learned to play the game to survive. She feels like she is in a bottle with a tight cap, wondering when she can come up for air or if anyone will untwist the cape so she can be free.

Life has a way of pulling the air out of the room, and anxiety loves to hog space in our hearts and minds. The what-ifs we play can make us feel helpless and powerless, and anger seems like a helpful tool to protect ourselves. Have you ever seen a wounded animal before? The animal could have its paw in a trap, its head stuck in between a tree, or limping down the road.

When people come near it, instead of welcoming the help, it turns to bite at the hand, attempting to bring healing. It is a foolish decision on behalf of the person who needs help to fight the person trying to help them. Ecclesiastes 7:9 says, "Be not quick in your spirit to become angry, for anger lodges in the heart of fools."

This reaction appears protective, but it could also be rooted in anger. They are angry because they are hurt in the first place. They were mad that they got themselves into this situation or that those who could have prevented it didn't. They want out but are trapped. Those who have to look at the caged bird also feel pain and, yes, sometimes anger.

Have you ever started thinking about an issue, and you got mad all over again? You began to fight in your thoughts, actions, or emotions. You

ANGER

wanted to throw punches, to kick, and scream, but none of that would change the outcome. The person you love would stay with an abuser. So, to process the pain, you can shift your emotions to anger. Always ready to pop off because you are not okay and you feel the offbeat effect on your heart.

But the magical question is, how do you get rid of it? How do you get rid of anger or help those battling with this spirit that easily masquerades as frustration, feistiness, being quick-tempered, or impatient? You have to block the pair that ushers in anger. This nasty duo is fear and anxiety.

I know it is easy to confuse the two and assume they mean the same thing: fear and anxiety. Yet, fear is a caution of danger, and anxiety is like the fear of perceived danger that may never manifest. I love how Pastor Stephen says it: anxiety is taking on the identity of fear. You don't just experience fear; you live in fear!

We may be unaware of how the power of faith, also known as willpower, can push our worst fears into the forefront. Whatever you think about, you can subconsciously usher into your life. Proverbs 23:7 says, "For as he thinketh in his heart, so is he: Eat and drink, saith he to thee; but his heart is not with thee."

What do you feel in your heart? Are you harboring pain, rejection, anger, anxiety, inferiority, powerlessness, or something else? How often do you search your heart? Most of us are in life, keeping busy so we don't have to search our hearts. We are present in the day, but we are absent in our hearts and minds from the activities we are performing. We are doing the work, but our hearts are far from it.

We have left our first love, and this is what

God has against us (Revelation 2:4). We have lost ourselves and abandoned the true glory we were formed in to believe lies the enemy has told us. We are in protective mode, and our body is on autopilot. We are doing what life requires, but we are not receiving what we need, and when someone is getting close to the parts of that heart, we respond like a wounded animal.

James 4:1-2 reads, "What causes quarrels, and what causes fights among you? Is it not this that your passions are at war within you? 2 You desire and do not have, so you murder. You covet and cannot obtain, so you fight and quarrel. You do not have because you do not ask."

Many of us are limping, walking around wounded and bleeding because we are not asking for what we need. We are only seeking to hide because we think hiding equals safety. We are not running to our Strong Tower but running from what can actually save us. Proverbs 18:10 says, "The name of the Lord is a strong tower; the righteous man runs into it and is safe."

When we reject the Word meant to encourage and guide us, a war happens within us. Our passion for having what we don't have turns to anger and causes us to be combative and unyielding because what we want, we cannot have. We may say I prayed, but are we patient and trust Yah over our desires, fears, cares, and ambitions?

If we allow the Father to have freedom in our lives, to see the good in the bad all the same, we can ease the itch to respond in anger when we don't have what we desire. A heart grows sick as we wait for what we pray for, and some of us get angry with Yah. The devil wants you to get offended, mad, angry, and take it out on yourself or someone else. We may not know that in our hearts, we blame God

ANGER

for our condition. We blame Him for our condition, and anger shows up to work out of our pain.

When we don't confess what is in our hearts to Yah, we find ourselves turning our backs on God. We are trying to heal without the healer. We are trying to defend ourselves and protect what we have left, only we are losing that which we attempted to save. He says that those who give their lives for My sake will save it; those who attempt to save it will lose it (Matthew 16:25)!

What we give to God, we are trusting Him with. Those who have pinned up anger have not trusted Him with their healing but are trying to self-medicate. They are trying to use a negative to hit another negative, thinking it will be positive, like math. But the equation has already been solved; you will only lose more of yourself and not gain with a heart like this.

You have to release this pain. You must be willing to experience your pain long enough so that you can hear others speak. We may need to tarry. He may require that we work before we get to work, and this could hurt us the most. We may be called, or those battling anger, to be slow to get angry because that quiets contention (Proverbs 15:8). If you want peace in your heart, you have to be a peacemaker because blessed are the peacemakers (Matthew 5:9).

We have to be willing to let go of our anger, wrath, malice, slander, and obscene talk from our mouths so we can change our heart position (Colossians 3:8). Conviction is what moves us to repentance. The anger in our hearts holds on to our disobedience to the Word. It is our thoughts that could appear to be healing and good that could lead to death (Proverbs 16:25).

RELEASE PAIN

We could be right in our own eyes to harbor anger, but anger, fire, held near our bosom will singe our hearts. It will change who we were designed to be. It will make us fall out of love with God and believe no one is good enough.

We can believe that others are not worthy of us. It can make a person lash out when people get close instead of giving them a loving embrace. With love and kindness has God drawn us, and as His children, we are to be harmless as doves and wise as serpents (Jeremiah 31:3, Galatians 3:26, Matthew 10:16). With this same heart, we must surrender our pain, our anger, our shame, our wounds, scars, and our sins.

We are all called to repentance no matter what others have done to us. Our retaliation is not made okay, or our treatment of others because of other people's actions. Psalms 7:11-12 says that "God is a righteous judge and a God who feels indignation every day. 12 If a man does not repent, God will whet His sword; He has bent and readied His bow."

The key to releasing anger is to allow conviction and repentance to take place in our hearts. For us to decrease to allow His power to increase (John 3:3). If you want God to enter into your heart or situation, to mute anger in your heart or someone else's, you have to be willing to put what you are owed in the Hands of Yah. He will repay all things, so don't worry about what you inflict on someone else, but trust that God is a just judge.

Choose to be free! Psalms 37:8-9 says to *Refrain from anger, and forsake wrath*! "Fret not yourself; it tends only to evil. 9 For the evildoers shall be cut off, but those who wait for the Lord shall inherit the land." If you and I learn to trust God with our pain, we can have confidence and not

ANGER

need anger to punish those who we feel deserve it. I can decrease so that Yah can increase in my heart and relationships. So I, we, have to refrain from anger and abandon wrath to keep evil out of our lives.

The reason evil has a foothold in our lives, or those we love, is because evil is tied to anger. "Loose lips sink ships," I heard growing up from my mother. Proverbs 15:1 says, "A soft answer turns away wrath, but a harsh word stirs up anger." When you connect that with Proverbs 29:1, "A fool gives full vent to his spirit, but a wise man quietly holds it back."

When the enemy talks to you and urges you to get even, to defend yourself, to fight, to snap back, and you choose not to, you are yielding the power of God! When you are doing things Yah wants you to do, there will be opposition. When you get pushback from people when you are trying to do right, don't leave your place of calm. Ecclesiastes 10:4 says, "If the anger of the ruler rises against you, do not leave your place, for calmness will lay great offenses to rest."

When you are steady in your emotions and intentions to do the work of God in your own heart, you are doing a great work. It is not sexy to follow God's ways above your natural instinct. You may not look like you are on top and rising fast. You may look like you are on a sinking ship, but God! He can speak to the wind. God can change the course of the water and steer you in a new direction.

No relationship, problem, or pain is too hard for Him to heal. When we exchange our anger for joy, we start to experience the calmness He asked for us to stand in. We cannot move too fast to get to what we want and skip the process of healing. Getting over it is not the same thing as healing.

RELEASE PAIN

When we have been hurt, the last thing we want to hear is, "Get over it. Worrying and thinking about it won't change anything." Although that may be true, burying our pain doesn't bring healing. If you have been stuck in suppressing pain, I want to give you a warm hug and tell you in your ear, "It's okay, sister or brother, we can release this to God. Open your heart and cry out to Him because He is concerned about you."

It is a deep feeling to know you have someone–not just anybody either, but the Creator of the Universe interested and invested in your life. He cares about you (1 Peter 5:7), what makes you feel pain, those who have hurt you, and the many you have hurt. The Father can restore you and everyone around you, no matter who is guilty within the circle.

As we change our hearts by doing the work to build with God, we won't see the vision clearly. We can miss our mark in life. We can feel out of place because our vision is too small. What we see is too small compared to what Yah had planned for us. We must elevate our stance. We must do the work with God to be brought to greater so we can see where we are going.

If you feel like you are blind, you don't know which way is up, it is time to build right where you are. We may know of the future, but not the road, so don't focus on where you can't see. Focus on building the foundation under your feet that you can stand on to get higher.

If you want stronger relationships, peace, harmony, love, and connection, you want to build the foundation. To see the higher heights, you must stabilize your base. No structure that hopes to stand can stand without good support underneath. Even a tree's roots are just as long underground as they

ANGER

stand above ground. You need to dig down deep within your heart, mind, body, soul, and spirit to have the reflection of that healing outwardly.

Don't skip this moment and invitation to go deep with God. Going deep doesn't mean hearing fancy words or hidden truth, but being willing to spend time with Yah to allow Him to renew your mind (Romans 12:2). "Do not be conformed to this world, but be transformed by the renewal of your mind, that by testing you may discern what the will of God is, what is good and acceptable and perfect."

We cannot respond like others do. We cannot respond anymore like how we feel. We cannot choose to deny the power of God in our lives and reap the benefits of His Presence. We must yield our power to the direction of God. We must trust Him with all that we have, the good and bad. We must lay our burdens down and trust Him to dispose of them and for Him to fill the holes they leave behind.

The enemy wants to step into the gaps in your life and bury seeds of anger, wrath, bitterness, hatred, and strife. He doesn't want peace but for all hell to break loose in your life. But you stay in your calm place. Find your prayer corner, closet, or time to speak with God and empty your heart of your concerns. Allow Father to do what He promises, to make your burdens lighter and your yoke easier (Matthew 11:28-30).

"Come to me, all who labor and are heavily laden, and I will give you rest. 29 Take my yoke upon you, and learn from me, for I am gentle and lowly in heart, and you will find rest for your souls. 30 For my yoke is easy, and my burden is light."

Be encouraged because as you start to get free, there are many who will bear witness to the change God is making in you. The changes the Word makes in us, the world sees it. People are watching how we respond and what we say and do in adversity. People, fallen angels, even the devil, along with witches and warlocks, watch you. But don't let that intimidate you.

Stay focused. Remain focused on the Word you have heard from Yah concerning what your burden is. If it is your marriage, trust His decision on the matter. If it is with your children, trust Him. In your finances, company, job, or career, allow Him to direct your path and give you rest. Sometimes, we lose to gain.

The Father can take you off one job, and give you months of time off to transition you for what is coming. Don't be anxious when you are in a waiting season. Enjoy the peace and calm, and focus on what you are to build in that season. Some of us are building and holding up the sword to fight with the other hand.

We are trying to lead our families but also waring in the spirit for our families. We are not building and working toward peace with no opposition but with skeptics, onlookers, and doubters spewing negative thoughts. We are battling on every side, but God! He is there with you during the storm. The Word is with you, fighting on your behalf as you pray and lean on him.

ANGER

The relationships you are building are so your grandchildren can use them. The company you are working for is for the inheritance of your children and grandchildren. The financial discipline you choose to learn is for the building of your legacy. Your willingness to hear others and make changes is because you want to do more than build a tower of your own. You want to join with Christ and build the Kingdom of God here on earth so others can enter it.

The same grace and mercy that will redeem you and those you pray for, you want to share with the world and those you have a burden to serve. The greatest among us serves (Matthew 23:11). Are you still willing to serve, or do you demand to be served solely? There is more for you and your family, so don't give up now.

Getting angry is losing hope in change. When we feel powerless to change things, anger is stepping into agreement with what we feel we cannot beat. We cannot overcome unrighteousness, unfairness, betrayal, pain, torment, and hurt, so we become it to survive. We disguise it, thinking deflection and denial bring power.

We need deliverance from the spirit of anger when we cannot spend a day without getting upset for one reason or another. There will always be a reason to step out of our peace, but our job and assignment is to stay in peace. I challenge you to consider what the Father has burdened you to change in your life, heart, or circumstances. Determine a way forward, and never give up on the vision that Yah gave you. Believe for it and work toward it because, with works behind your faith, you can move mountains.

Let's wrap this up with the close. But before I go, I want to share these scriptures and power statements.

EMPOWERING SCRIPTURES: INJUSTICE

Proverbs 17:28 Even a fool who keeps silent is considered wise; when he closes his lips, he is deemed intelligent.

Romans 3:23 for all have sinned and fall short of the glory of God,

Romans 12:20 To the contrary, "if your enemy is hungry, feed him; if he is thirsty, give him something to drink; for by so doing you will heap burning coals on his head."

Matthew 5:46 For if you love those who love you, what reward do you have? Do not even the tax collectors do the same?

Romans 12:19 Beloved, never avenge yourselves, but leave it to the wrath of God, for it is written, "Vengeance is mine, I will repay, says the Lord."

Galatians 3:13 Christ redeemed us from the curse of the law by becoming a curse for us—for it is written, "Cursed is everyone who is hanged on a tree"—

Matthew 7:1-2 Judge not, that you be not judged. 2 For with the judgment you pronounce you will be judged, and with the measure you use it will be measured to you.

Matthew 5:38 You have heard that it was

ANGER

said, 'An eye for an eye and a tooth for a tooth.

Proverbs 16:25 There is a way that seems right to a man, but its end is the way to death.

Matthew 5:38-39 "You have heard that it was said, 'An eye for an eye and a tooth for a tooth.' 39 But I say to you, Do not resist the one who is evil. But if anyone slaps you on the right cheek, turn to him the other also.

Matthew 7:1-2 Judge not, that you be not judged. 2 For with the judgment you pronounce you will be judged, and with the measure you use it will be measured to you.

1 Samuel 16:7 But the Lord said to Samuel, "Do not look on his appearance or on the height of his stature, because I have rejected him. For the Lord sees not as man sees: man looks on the outward appearance, but the Lord looks on the heart."

Matthew 5:38-39 "You have heard that it was said, 'An eye for an eye and a tooth for a tooth.' 39 But I say to you, Do not resist the one who is evil. But if anyone slaps you on the right cheek, turn to him the other also.

Matthew 23:11 The greatest among you shall be your servant.

Romans 12:2 Do not be conformed to this world, but be transformed by the renewal of your mind, that by testing you may discern what is the will of God, what is good and acceptable and perfect.

1 Peter 5:7 Casting all your anxieties on him, because he cares for you.

John 3:30 He must increase, but I must

decrease."

Galatians 3:26 for in Christ Jesus you are all sons of God, through faith.

1 John 3:1 See what kind of love the Father has given to us, that we should be called children of God; and so we are. The reason why the world does not know us is that it did not know him.

Jeremiah 31:3 The LORD hath appeared of old unto me, saying, Yea, I have loved thee with an everlasting love: therefore with loving kindness have I drawn thee".

Proverbs 23:7 For as he thinketh in his heart, so is he: Eat and drink, saith he to thee; but his heart is not with thee.
Revelation 2:4 But I have this against you, that you have abandoned the love you had at first.

Proverbs 18:10 The name of the Lord is a strong tower; the righteous man runs into it and is safe.

Matthew 16:25 "For whoever would save his life[a] will lose it, but whoever loses his life for my sake will find it."

Matthew 5:9 Blessed are the peacemakers, for they shall be called sons of God.

Luke 15:25-30 - 25 "Now his older son was in the field, and as he came and drew near to the house, he heard music and dancing. 26 And he called one of the servants and asked what these things meant.

27 And he said to him, 'Your brother has come, and your father has killed the fattened calf because he has received him back safe and sound.' 28 But he

ANGER

was angry and refused to go in. His father came out and entreated him,

29 but he answered his father, 'Look, these many years I have served you, and I never disobeyed your command, yet you never gave me a young goat, that I might celebrate with my friends. 30 But when this son of yours came, who has devoured your property with prostitutes, you killed the fattened calf for him!'

Proverbs 19:11 Good sense makes one slow to anger, and it is his glory to overlook an offense.

James 1:19-20 Know this, my beloved brothers: let every person be quick to hear, slow to speak, slow to anger; 20 for the anger of man does not produce the righteousness of God.

Ecclesiastes 7:9 Be not quick in your spirit to become angry, for anger lodges in the hearing of fools.

Proverbs 15:1 A soft answer turns away wrath, but a harsh word stirs up anger.

Proverbs 29:11 A fool gives full vent to his spirit, but a wise man quietly holds it back. Proverbs 15:18 A hot-tempered man stirs up strife, but he who is slow to anger quiets contention.

Colossians 3:8 But now you must put them all away: anger, wrath, malice, slander, and obscene talk from your mouth.

James 4:1-2 What causes quarrels, and what causes fights among you? Is it not this, that your passions are at war within you? 2 You desire and do not have, so you murder. You covet and cannot obtain, so you fight and quarrel. You do not have to because you do not ask.

RELEASE PAIN

Romans 5:8 But God shows his love for us in that while we were still sinners, Christ died for us.

Romans 12:20 To the contrary, "if your enemy is hungry, feed him; if he is thirsty, give him something to drink; for by so doing you will heap burning coals on his head." 21 Do not be overcome by evil, but overcome evil with good.

Luke 23:34 And Jesus said, "Father, forgive them, for they know not what they do." And they cast lots to divide his garments.

1 Corinthians 13:4 Love is patient and kind; love does not envy or boast; it is not arrogant

1 John 4:8 Anyone who does not love does not know God, because God is love.

Psalms 37:8-9 Refrain from anger, and forsake wrath! Fret not yourself; it tends only to evil. 9 For the evildoers shall be cut off, but those who wait for the Lord shall inherit the land.

Psalms 7:11-12 God is a righteous judge, and a God who feels indignation every day. 12 If a man does not repent, God will whet his sword; he has bent and readied his bow;

I Corinthians 13:4-7 Love is patient and kind; love does not envy or boast; it is not arrogant 5 or rude. It does not insist on its own way; it is not irritable or resentful; 6 it does not rejoice at wrongdoing, but rejoices with the truth. 7 Love bears all things, believes all things, hopes all things, endures all things.

ANGER

YOUR POWER AND FOUNDATION

When we get something we don't deserve, we can feel gratitude. It's nice when someone throws you a lifeline when you are sinking deep. We try to watch the bubbles to see where the top is located based on where they float, but when it is dark around us, even the bubbles seem to blend in with our surroundings.

For some of us, our choices have led us to live a life of isolation and honestly out of fear. We fought to protect ourselves so we don't become a victim anymore, but now we can find ourselves wearing the shoes of the victimizer. We may see that we are not perfect like we thought we once were, but we have been blaming others for the change and shooing away our accountability.

When we are tired of running, we can be like the prodigal son who wanted what he felt he deserved. In Luke, the parable of the son who wished his father dead to get his inheritance got what he prayed for. He got the money, and he left home thinking to spend it how he wanted to. He spent the money on people who didn't love him, who were not his friends, and when his money was gone, they quickly abandoned him.

Have you found yourself believing lies about your actions? For those constantly angry, who feel wronged, and like they are owed something from not just one person but everyone for their pain. They can wish away everyone from their presence, not realizing they are isolating themselves from those who could also help them.

The prodigal thought he needed what he was owed at that moment to be happy and to be made whole. Yet, he was the most whole when he was at home, himself, and in his right mind. When we are angry, our thoughts can mislead us. We can speak quickly and not worry about who we send packing. Someone dealing with anger could be quick to yell or fight with you, making you run for the hills justified.

But like in the prodigal son, when this person, and if it is you, find themselves alone, pray to be humbled. When you hurt people like this son hurt his father, turn the check of retaliation. Pray that your heart or their heart will be softened. The prodigal, as he was eating slop with pigs, realized he didn't have to be there. He could go home to a place where he was loved and appreciated.

You may need to go to a place where you are loved, where you feel happy and content, and that leaves a lighter impression about life for you. People can do cruel things, people can be mean, and those who should have loved you can abuse or misuse you. Yes, that is true. However, don't give away your power to have joy, to be happy, and to have peace in your heart and mind because of other people. Not even to a spirit that would convince you that being alone is the best place to be. That hating others will somehow set you free.

When the prodigal son went home, he wasn't trying to come back as a son but would have been fine to be a servant of his father. He knew his father was a good man to help him, so he wanted a job because he already blew his portion of the money. When his dad saw him far off, he didn't greet him like a stranger. He didn't send him away or reject him because of how he was treated.

ANGER

He instead hugged him. So many people today need a hug and not a strong rebuke. Life has beat them down. Spirits have held them down, and they are looking for some relief from the storm. The storm that swirls pain, memories, and even shame from decisions they made or had to live through could melt away.

As the son was being embraced, onlookers thought it was wonderful at the moment. Some thought the dad was crazy when he said to prepare this big party and spend money for his son's return. Is this not an example of the father given his son his cloak after he took the money? Is this not like him turning the other check to expose himself again to the potential disappointment from his son? His eldest son was one who had strong opinions of his father's treatment to welcome his younger son.

He complained about all the money being spent when the younger son had already used his portion. That was another slap to the father's face. For some of us, everyone who should be happy about you coming home will not be. Out of anger they might not be able to be happy for you or someone else. Some will think you don't deserve nothing because you burnt bridges. Some will say what someone did was to terrible, and although it can be forgiven, it should never be forgotten but remain lodged as a forever offense.

There are those who argue that a woman shouldn't have a baby shower for her unborn based on the circumstances of her pregnancy. These forever offenses pose stumbling blocks and could make us pray things we shouldn't. It can make us say things that are too harsh to God.

We serve a merciful God who loves the prodigal and the faithful son or daughter. I want to encourage those who have burned bridges to know it is not over. For those who have had to live through unspeakable acts that have left them in pain, who are angry, and fighting for the last bit of sanity they have, hold on.

What we need to overcome anger is LOVE. I know it sounds simple. You may say I don't need love, I don't even want it. But God is love, and everything He has created is good and was created in Love (1 John 4:8).

This is the gel, the glue that connects us to one another. With love and kindness has He drawn us. Love is not an emotion, a thought, or a feeling, although it impacts these three things. Love is action, responses, mercy, grace, forgiveness, and healing. Love is patient and kind; love does not envy or boast; it is not arrogant (1 Corinthians 13:4). Love allows us to celebrate the wins of those who hurt us.

I remember when my second husband couldn't remain faithful. It led ultimately to our divorce. He was young and perhaps too young for the level of commitment I required to be in a relationship. However, while we were separated and waiting on paperwork to finalize our divorce, he had another relationship that brought forth more family.

I wasn't mad when I heard about it, in fact, I prayed for them. I wanted this family to work if it could because mine not working shouldn't mean he has to repeat what happened with us. I prayed for that not to be the case and although I don't know the details, he is now working diligently to bring his children together and become a better person for them all.

I celebrate the fact that he is trying to build and maintain a healthy relationship with our sons and his third child. I do care about her having a re-

ANGER

lationship with her brothers. I can love a baby that should have brought me pain. It makes me smile to see my sons talk, walk, laugh, and act like their father. Their loving challenges bring back some of the happy memories of their father to me. It's okay to enjoy the good and pray for the things that need to change.

When we allow our pain to turn into prayer, we bring Yah into our hearts and allow Him to work not just on them but on us, too. I felt I didn't deserve or wouldn't find what I was looking for. I questioned if it was me, my picker, or what I demanded out of life. The truth was that I was in pain for a few years, and although I knew the marriage was over a year or two years prior, I wanted to win at this.

My anger about the end didn't result in fighting or bitterness, but it did lead to me having bouts of self-loathing. I didn't want to think about a relationship anymore. I stopped praying for one, and today, I have my moments where I am completely disinterested. I have to ask, is that because of my fear of picking wrong again or because I honestly desire to be set apart, single, to work the ministry I was called to live?

I still am praying about the outcome of my marriage life and one day, I may have an answer, but I don't want my past relationships, failures, pains, or heartbreaks to creep in and make me angry enough to block out what God could have for me. I would encourage anyone who has been hurt, assaulted, abused, or treated harshly by someone else–it could be a parent, to find it in their hearts to forgive. To pray for yourself and them.

I know it is not easy to pray for those who hurt you or to think of something nice. I know on the cross, it would be natural for Yashua/Jesus to hate the people who put Him there. BUT! He prayed and said, "Father, forgive them, for they know not what they do" (Luke 23:34). Some people will never fathom the pain they caused you, and it takes God to soften their heart to see it. It is not our job to make someone feel our pain by inflicting it back, or for us to seek our own vengeance.

When we are kind to those who were not kind to us, that is when we have the greatest reward. Romans 12:20-21 says, "To the contrary, "if your enemy is hungry, feed him; if he is thirsty, give him something to drink; for by so doing you will heap burning coals on his head." 21 Do not be overcome by evil, but overcome evil with good."

We do not want to be overcome by evil, by anger, or by doing wrong because we were wronged. When we do good, we offer up hope and love that can overcome a multitude of offenses. If you need to change your heart so you can be a better parent, teacher, business owner, believer, or example, begin with doing good to all, understanding that it was first done for you. While we were still sinners, Christ died to save, redeem humanity (Romans 5:8). The deepest love is shown when we care when it is undeserved or not summoned.

ANGER

LOVE

As we release pain in our lives, love will be what pushes it out. If you are in pain or ditching it out, love can heal and restore you. The same power that can heal the victim can restore the heart of the victimizer. No one is perfect, and all men have fallen short of the glory, the promise, and intent for humanity God has (Romans 3:23).

I want to empower you to explore Yah's greater plan for us. Where you are now isn't where you have to remain. The Father can redeem your time, making your latter days greater than the former (Job 8:7). The Bible talks about how *light momentary affliction is preparing for us an eternal weight of glory beyond all comparison* (1 Corinthians 4:17). No matter what has been done, none of it is bigger than the power of God to heal you. To make you whole again–even better than before.

The pain or shame you have held all this time can be placed in the Hands of Yah, and He can work it out for you! Romans 13:9 says, "The commandments, 'You shall not commit adultery, you shall not murder, you shall not steal, you shall not covet,' and whatever other commandment there may be, are summed up in this one command: 'Love your neighbor as yourself. The greatest commandment sums up the others. Love your neighbor "others" as yourself.

RELEASE PAIN

Love is the most powerful sword, tool, or getback you can muster. To get back at the enemy and stop him in his tracks, show love. It is not always easy to be a soldier for God because His weapons are not carnal but mighty to pull down strongholds (2 Corinthians 10:4).

To love, when it is far easier to hate, is a weapon from heaven and not a device of the devil. He hates love, goodness, mercy, and kindness. He loves judgment, robbery, hatred, anger, injustice, lying, betrayal, jealousy, envy, and vengeance. We put hot coals on his head when we do good to those who mistreat us. We go through the fire, and we are purified by our actions and hearts to be like Christ.

We are not doormats, victims, slaves, idiots, or mindless faith talkers. We are powerful beings who can see past a person's current condition and shape a world with our words, which can change everything. We are stronger than wizards, witches, warlocks, the occult, and the elite. When the Kingdom gets together to accomplish a great work that the Father says yes to, nothing can come against you and prosper (Isaiah 54:17).

We do have a set amount of time that only God knows. What is in our control is how we spend our time. What we decide to focus on is what becomes the most important. Although the darkness can be thick. The deep pain, the injustice, the robbery, betrayal, the hatred, the lies, the sabotage, the anger, the light shines in the darkness and is not overcome by it (John 1:5)! Yah can take on your pain and keep it from consuming you.

Trust Him with your pain, healing, and deliverance. Finally, I will leave you with the last set of empowering scriptures meant to encourage you through this journey to release pain. There is a passage that I felt needed more than a singular reference. To quote it in part was not justice to what it can do to reshape life for you and those you love. Join me in Psalm 37.

This translation is ESV, as it has been throughout the entire book, but pick the version that best helps you understand the promises of God concerning you! He didn't bring you this far to leave you, and although you have pain, He is able to reach in deep and pull you out! He has the final say and is the Way to the Truth and the Good Life (John 14:16)!

What makes us do something so radical to love those who hate us? To be good even when others around us are not? To be just when those we watch get away with murder and injustice? Here is our confidence:

EMPOWERING SCRIPTURES: LOVE

John 14:6 Jesus said to him, "I am the way, and the truth, and the life. No one comes to the Father except through me.

Job 8:7 And though your beginning was small, your latter days will be very great.

Romans 3:23 For all have sinned and fall short of the glory of God,

2 Corinthians 4:17 For this light momentary affliction is preparing for us an eternal weight of glory beyond all comparison,

2 Corinthians 10:4 For the weapons of our

warfare are not of the flesh but have divine power to destroy strongholds.

Romans 13:9 The commandments, 'You shall not commit adultery, you shall not murder, you shall not steal, you shall not covet,' and whatever other commandment there may be, are summed up in this one command: 'Love your neighbor as yourself.'

YOUR POWER AND FOUNDATION

I could not end this book without encouraging you with a powerful Psalm that needs no introduction. Psalm 37 was dropped into my heart to close this book as I wrote chapter three. I knew the ending clearly. We need to have the confidence that we are on the winning side no matter what we may have to endure to reach the other side.

You are empowered to do all things through Christ who strengthens you! May this closing scripture bless you and keep you encouraged as you journey through the necessary changes in your life to align with the will of Yah for your life. Shalom, peace, and blessings from my heart to yours. Lastly, I will leave you with some resources, and then we will say bye-bye for now.

RELEASE PAIN

1 Fret not yourself because of evildoers; be not envious of wrongdoers!
2 For they will soon fade like the grass and wither like the green herb.

3 Trust in the Lord, and do good; dwell in the land and befriend faithfulness.
4 Delight yourself in the Lord, and He will give you the desires of your heart.

5 Commit your way to the Lord; trust in Him, and He will act.
6 He will bring forth your righteousness as the light, and your justice as the noonday.

7 Be still before the Lord and wait patiently for Him; fret not yourself over the one who prospers in his way, over the man who carries out evil devices!
8 Refrain from anger, and forsake wrath! Fret not yourself; it tends only to evil.

9 For the evildoers shall be cut off, but those who wait for the Lord shall inherit the land.
10 In just a little while, the wicked will be no more; though you look carefully at his place, he will not be there.

RELEASE PAIN

11 But the meek shall inherit the land and delight themselves in abundant peace.
12 The wicked plots against the righteous and gnashes his teeth at him,

13 but the Lord laughs at the wicked, for He sees that His day is coming.
14 The wicked draw the sword and bend their bows to bring down the poor and needy, to slay those whose way is upright;

15 their sword shall enter their own heart, and their bows shall be broken.
16 Better is the little that the righteous has than the abundance of many wicked.

17 For the arms of the wicked shall be broken, but the Lord upholds the righteous.
18 The Lord knows the days of the blameless, and their heritage will remain forever;

19 they are not put to shame in evil times; in the days of famine they have abundance.
20 But the wicked will perish; the enemies of the Lord are like the glory of the pastures; they vanish—like smoke they vanish away.

RELEASE PAIN

21 The wicked borrows but does not pay back, but the righteous is generous and gives;
22 for those blessed by the Lord shall inherit the land, but those cursed by Him shall be cut off.

23 The steps of a man are established by the Lord, when he delights in his way;
24 though he fall, he shall not be cast headlong, for the Lord upholds his hand.

25 I have been young, and now am old, yet I have not seen the righteous forsaken or His children begging for bread.
26 He is ever lending generously, and His children become a blessing.

27 Turn away from evil and do good; so shall you dwell forever.
28 For the Lord loves justice; He will not forsake His saints. They are preserved forever,
but the children of the wicked shall be cut off.

29 The righteous shall inherit the land and dwell upon it forever.
30 The mouth of the righteous utters wisdom, and his tongue speaks justice.

RELEASE PAIN

31 The law of his God is in his heart; his steps do not slip.
32 The wicked watches for the righteous and seeks to put him to death.

33 The Lord will not abandon him to his power or let him be condemned when he is brought to trial.
34 Wait for the Lord and keep His way, and He will exalt you to inherit the land;
you will look on when the wicked are cut off.

35 I have seen a wicked, ruthless man, spreading himself like a green laurel tree.
36 But he passed away, and behold, he was no more; though I sought him, he could not be found.

37 Mark the blameless and behold the upright, for there is a future for the man of peace.
38 But transgressors shall be altogether destroyed; the future of the wicked shall be cut off.

39 The salvation of the righteous is from the Lord; He is their stronghold in the time of trouble.
40 The Lord helps them and delivers them; He delivers them from the wicked and saves them, because they take refuge in Him.

LOVE

Congratulations on completing this book. Words cannot express not only my gratitude but my expectations for how this book will impact your life as you begin to engage with the elements of change. it will be completely impossible for you to invite Yah/God into your life and He not change you from the inside out.

I know, for some of us, the pain we have held on to for years is not so easy to let go of. We can think and strongly battle to make the necessary changes to empower our lives and release pain. We know that pain gives our dark adversaries access to us, but that doesn't mean we don't want to struggle with the devil we know rather than deal with the fear of the unknown.

Pain can bring comfort, ironically, and we can find pain more familiar than freedom and love. I don't want you to be persuaded that your release from pain is a one-and-done thing. This is a life commitment to release any pain that tries to rise up against you today, tomorrow, next month, and throughout the years to come. I know it is a battle to stay on the right side when the enemy offers shortcuts to feel good.

Don't take the bait and turn away from a steadfast love and a peace that surpasses all understanding. It is a trick that we may have fallen for time and time again, but I believe that this time can be different for you. The Father can make you whole, but do you want it? Are you willing to protect the relationship you are forming or growing with God on a regular basis?

I want to encourage you that this journey is one you can take with the safety of friends and the body of Christ. I encourage you to get a healthy church family circle about you. Not everyone is the same, and unfortunately, we can come across bad and unfruitful ones, same as the anointed and Holy Spirit-filled ones.

If you need help finding a church home, I have some free tips provided on my site: AuthorKLee.com that I found helpful and want to share with you. I also want to provide you with a weekly book club: "Growing Book Club," that you can join and stay connected with other believers. It is important that you keep holy friends and those who can love you and give you a safe space. This group can do that and provides more powerful and fun reads to keep you light and focused on what matters in life. Go to KLeeEvents.com to learn more.

As for my recommended Book List, here are some books to get you going.

Devotionals:
Bless the Works of My Hands: 21-Day Devotional and Journal

Spiritually Guided Books:
The Biggest Mistake Can Cost You Everything
The Ecstasy You Want Heaven But Won't Give Up Hell

Books to Read to Your Children:
The Day of Worship
Put Your Helmet On

Books for Your Husband:
The Rise and Fall of King Saul
The Biggest Mistake Can Cost You Everything

Books for Your Teenager:
The Lesson Series: Personal Development, Blended Families, and 8 other titles.

New Believer Book:
Over the Fact

Season Believer:
Look For the Drip and Expect the Outpour

New Business Owner:
Turn Key Solution: Go From Dreaming to Paid - a series of Guides to Help You Start or Grow Your Business.
Write Anything Easily - a series of Guides to Help You Write, Format, and Publish Your book!

Those Dealing with Inadequacy:
Embrace Your Crown Series: Overcome Heartbreak, Overcome Unbelief, Sharpen Your Focus

Books to Help with Depression:
Be Happy: Keys to Think Yourself Happy

Seniors & Old Age: Memory Loss Dementia
Faithful Heart

Novels:
We Expect the Drip and Not the Downpour
Alone...But Never Lonely: Katherine

    Lastly, I want to share the sister book with this one. In the next book, I wanted to present the Devil's Evil Plan for our lives and why he wants our pain. What makes him seek to keep us pinned in pain? What is his endgame for using our pain, and how does it impact our lives if we refuse to release it?

I know that everyone, unfortunately, won't implement what was presented in this book. It may be too tempting to go back to familiar spirits than to not only "Try Jesus" but to make the Word the foundation of our lives. It took us years to get where we are; for some of us, deliverance could be the same length of time.

If you find yourself on the fence about whether this is what you want to do or if you want to know the devil's plan so you can pray and serve in the ministry to cover other saints as they travel this road, I encourage you to get this book. This book, The Devil's Evil Plan, is a must-read and must-have for evangelism, helping others who would not choose a church experience and those who are not certain Yah is real or big enough to solve their problems.

"Taste Yah and know He is good!" But some of us are too afraid, shamed, or unbelieving to try Yashua, Jesus. We will get excited but then allow the fallen angels to steal our Word, the seed sent to heal our pain. It's okay if you are battling to give things to God; He can handle your honesty. However, can you handle--or those who would turn their backs on Him, the repercussions of making that decision? I want to encourage you to know why you want to release your pain and stay free! Or encourage the babies in Christ and the reprobates to return home.

This book is not about religion and a red devil with a pitchfork; this book will show the unraveling of people's lives and answer the question many ask and want to know, "Why?" Get this hot release by ordering with the QR or at AuthorKLee.com.

THE DEVIL'S PLAN

K. Lee

Before the Father judges something, He will send His prophet or a preacher to give a warning concerning the choices people have made. We can hear the warning and still set our feet on living a life of hell. We can choose to fight a battle we are destined to lose and enjoy the hell we endure on the journey to fame, fortune, owning things, or rising to high esteem.

We can believe that the things the devil offers us in exchange for our soul: mind, will, and emotions are a small price to pay to enjoy the benefits of being a conduit of hell on earth!

I assure you that the Devil's Evil Plan for every life is not so easy to go along with. The heart will cry out for Love to the Heavenly Creator, but will His voice be muted so humanity can continue in the footsteps of hell? Just what are the devil's plans for those who won't ***Release Pain*** anyway? Shouldn't we know the truth? The Father of Lies will never give us the Truth because it is not in him, but the Father of Light will expose the Devil's Evil Plan to bring hell here on earth!

Allow me to explain...

AUTHOR

> "God blesses those who work for peace, for they will be called the children of God."
> Matthew 5:9

Krystal Lee is proud to have authored this book and accompanying course to better readers' lives. She has a heart for helping people in their deepest times of need. She writes because she believes there is power in sharing stories and life accounts that others can benefit from and learn from.

Sharing is caring, so she shares stories, ideas, and resources to better the lives of her readers.

In addition, Dr. Lee has authored over 35 books across twelve or more genres (adult, children, youth fiction, self-help, spiritual growth, novels, how-to guides, and more), in addition to ghostwriting and editing more than 20 published works. She has launched coaching programs and web courses that helped formulate many startup companies. Her specialty is aiding coaches, creatives, and service-based companies in defining their message, brand, unique selling point, and client avatar, as well as generating a sales cycle and structure for her clients.

Empowering individuals is at the core of her work, and she is driven by her passion to continue writing. In addition to being an author, Krystal Lee is a business owner of multiple companies, a consultant, an ordained minister and chaplain, and a public speaker.

For more information about Dr. Krystal Lee, scan the QR.

To engage with the Coaching series and Monthly Meet up Group for Embrace Your Crown First Sundays at 4pm, please use the QR or visit InviteEyc.com and EmbraceYourCrown.com

AuthorKLee.com
Creator of
WAE Process

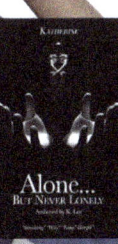

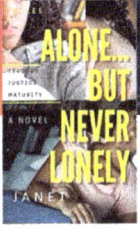

Explore and learn more about published authors affiliated with KLE.

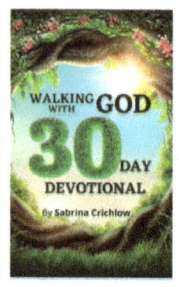

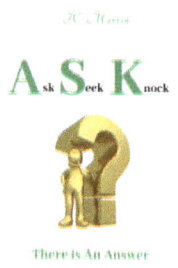

KLEPub.com

SCAN ME

Call or Text:
770-240-0089 Press Extension 1
Web: KLEpub.com
Email Services@klepub.com

It's time to start and finish **YOUR Story!**

KLE Publishing specializes in helping people become authors. In as little as 15 to 90 days, we can help you develop your books and e-books and publish to 39,000 outlets! We also offer audiobook services.

Write, Edit, Format, Publish
We can help from
Start to Finish.

RELEASE PAIN